Frontispiece

Some of the material contained herein is taken from a Taylor & Francis article entitled: "The March from Selma to Montgomery and the Nonviolent Movement in Analysis," Psychological Perspectives, Los Angeles, California, Vol. 61, 2018, pp. 331–343.

Book cover painting by
Zachariah Collins

"This book is a study of the history of the racial dilemma in the United States. It includes the Civil Rights Movement and its leaders, such as Martin Luther King. It amplifies the theory of non-violence by using some of the writings of Gandhi and King and others. This work is important in studying the healing of psychological splitting, and I highly recommend it for any reader who is curious about these topics and is willing to think symbolically and metaphorically about them."

—**Ben F. Toole**, Jungian Analyst, USA

"In the face of the worldwide epidemic of violence, this book is historically timely. Renée Cunningham offers an important alternative to violence by demonstrating the value of the spiritual practice of nonviolence. The book's focus on the psychological underpinnings of nonviolence contributes to a greater understanding of exactly why nonviolence can be so effective."

—**Lionel Corbett,** MD, Jungian Analyst, Pacifica Graduate Institute, USA

"From the consulting room to the political scene we search for a container to hold the tension of the opposites. Following the path of nonviolence so aptly described by this author gives us the opportunity to experience and grow from this tension."

—**Billye Bob Currie**, Jungian Analyst, USA

Archetypal Nonviolence

Renée Moreau Cunningham's unique study utilizes the psychology of C. G. Jung and the spiritual teachings of Mahatma Gandhi and Martin Luther King, Jr. to explore how nonviolence works psychologically as a form of spiritual warfare, confronting and transmuting aggression.

Archetypal Nonviolence uses King's iconic march from Selma to Montgomery, a demonstration which helped introduce America to nonviolent philosophy on a mass scale, as a metaphor for psychological and spiritual activism on an individual and collective level. Cunningham's work explores the core wound of racism in America on both a collective and a personal level, investigating how we hide from our own potential for evil and how the divide within ourselves can be bridged. The book demonstrates that the alchemical transmutation of aggression through a nonviolent ethos, as shown in the Selma marches, is important to understand as a beginning to something greater within the paradox of human violence and its bedfellow, nonviolence.

Archetypal Nonviolence explores how we can truly transform hatred by understanding how it operates within. It will be of great interest to Jungian analysts and analytical psychologists in practice and in training, and to academics and students of Jungian and post-Jungian studies, American history, race and racism, and nonviolent movements.

Renée Moreau Cunningham is a Diplomate Jungian Analyst of the Inter-Regional Society of Jungian Analysts, Texas Chapter. She is a licensed Marriage and Family Therapist who has been in private practice for over twenty-seven years.

Archetypal Nonviolence

King, Jung, and Culture Through
the Eyes of Selma

Renée Moreau Cunningham, MFT

Routledge
Taylor & Francis Group
LONDON AND NEW YORK

First published 2021
by Routledge
2 Park Square, Milton Park, Abingdon, Oxon OX14 4RN

and by Routledge
52 Vanderbilt Avenue, New York, NY 10017

Routledge is an imprint of the Taylor & Francis Group, an informa business

© 2021 Renée Moreau Cunningham

British Library Cataloguing in Publication Data
A catalogue record for this book is available from the British Library

Library of Congress Cataloging-in-Publication Data
A catalog record has been requested for this book

ISBN: 978-0-367-11224-0 (hbk)
ISBN: 978-0-367-11226-4 (pbk)
ISBN: 978-0-429-02541-9 (ebk)

Typeset in Times New Roman
by Taylor & Francis Books

To Scott, for keeping the light on...

Contents

Figures

Acknowledgments

The production of this book is due to the commitment of many people who have supported this endeavor. Thank you, Linda for your dreams and the sharing of parts of yourself in this book, which provide insight for all of us struggling to be understood by the other. I owe a huge debt of gratitude to Susan Rowland, Monika Wickman and Karen Hodges for suggesting and supporting this book's publication. To Lionel Corbett, Billye-Bobb Currie, Ben and Donna Toole for their time, professional commitment and belief in the power of nonviolence. As Southerners, Billye and Ben give depth to the material through their vulnerability and continued wish for change in the greater South and in the country in general. I thank Ron Schenk for pushing me deeper into myself in the writing of the material. For their conversations and input, I thank Clayborne Carson, David Garrow, Sam Kimbles, Michael Vannoy Adams, Fanny Brewster, Mark Winborn, Laura Chapman, and Donna Robinson. Thank you to my editor at Routledge, Susannah Frearson for her faith and support in this project.

This book is an alchemical birth born from a childhood defined by the Vietnam War, racism in the South and the civil rights movement. My training as an analyst brought to bear the significant, ongoing complexes which defined my country then and now and continues to influence my own psyche as I further my becoming into a spiritual human being. To this end, there are all of those supervising and training analysts to thank at the Inter-Regional Society of Jungian Analysts; particularly those in the Texas and New Mexico chapters. Thank you to Susan Schwartz for always pointing the way. I thank Jacqueline West and Barry Williams for fortifying my anxiety and periods of despair with focus, purpose, hope and love. Finally, to my beautiful family: Scott, Carly and Max, I thank you for your love, humor, and honesty. And to my birth family, thank you for your ongoing support.

Introduction

The clock above the Tallahatchie County Courthouse in Sumner, Mississippi is frozen at five minutes to twelve. The courthouse has long been shuttered, chained and deserted as evidenced by the spider webs clinging to the bars that frame the stairs leading up and into the courtroom. The courthouse stands in the center of the deserted square.

The surrounding stores are deserted except for one, a restaurant, while opened for business, is also empty. There are no humans present but for the few of us who have come to the Delta to pay tribute to Emmett Till, a fourteen-year-old African American boy, who had been beaten, shot and lynched in Money, Mississippi on August 28, 1955.

While it is September 2018, I feel as if I have stepped into a timeless void. The lifeforce of the town itself has been sucked dry, leaving only a petrified, pitiful shell of buildings and streets. It is here in summer, over fifty years earlier that Roy Bryant and his half-brother Milam celebrated their freedom when an all-male, all-white jury acquitted them for the lynching death of Emmett Till on September 23, 1955. While they and their wives smiled for the cameras, the outraged country began protesting the jury's decision. The acquittal also sparked what would become a general outrage over a multitude of unsolved, racially related murders which defined Bryant and Milam's beloved Delta, and the greater American South.

It was only a few weeks earlier that Emmett Till's distraught and shocked mother buckled over the badly mutilated body of her son. During the viewing, Mamie Till Bradley demanded that the undertaker keep the casket open: "let the world see what they did to my boy" (Anderson, 2015, p. 56). With this request, she not only committed the ultimate nonviolent move, but she had sacrificed her son's dignity for the sake of the country, laying bare the vilest part of the split American psyche, and demanding reconciliation. Emmett had been beaten and shot, his face mutilated by acid. He wore a ring bearing his father's initials, the only means of making his true identity evident. The body was so badly decomposed that a glass pane had to be placed over the body to shield the public from the smell. The amount of rage required to construct such an act is unfathomable to many Americans, but in

Mississippi in 1955, a racist backlash fueled a string of murders that broke out across the South and in Mississippi, triggered in part by *Brown vs. the Board of Education* (1954), which banned segregation in educational institutions (Anderson, 2015, p. 25).

The nonviolent stand Bradley took for her beloved son Emmett would be repeated less than three months later in Montgomery, Alabama when an African American woman, Rosa Parks refused to give up her seat on a bus to a white person. Ms. Parks was a member of a newly formed organization in her church, named The Montgomery Improvement Association, led by the church's newly minted pastor, Martin Luther King, Jr. Together, Mamie Bradley, Rosa Parks, and Martin Luther King, Jr. were three individuals who solidified and crystallized the nation's emerging civil rights movement, with Emmett Till's death serving as the historical flashpoint which altered the spiritual landscape of racism in America, yet again.

Mamie Till Bradley could not have anticipated the power of her nonviolent act, or the chapter of American history her decision would set into motion. Twelve o'clock symbolizes the passing over from day into night, good into evil, one cycle of life ending, and another beginning; Dr. Martin Luther King, Jr. stated "… the deep darkness of the midnight is interrupted by the sound of a knock … it is midnight in the moral order" (King, 2014, p. 349).

Mamie Till Bradley's call for justice would be answered, but not without more death's and great suffering for many people. In the moment of her unbearable agony, she could not foresee that eight years later on the anniversary of her son's death, Dr. King would deliver an homage to her son in his "I Have a Dream" speech, which ushered in a new, inclusive vision of freedom for children of all colors.

The civil rights movement has had a profound effect on the nation's consciousness at large and has shaped the American experience. For more than thirteen years, from 1955 to 1968, the country wrestled with the long-standing psychological split within the American psyche; a split formed around racism. Racism is an old and ever-changing story in our national narrative reflecting a central complex of the American psyche. This complex of racism is a kaleidoscopic, affective experience based on one's familial, cultural and ancestral roots. At the core of the complex lies the archetypal relationship of the master and the slave, a wound essentially defined by the paradigm of power, dominance and submission.

America and the Constitution on which it is based are birthed of the archetype of democracy, the dream of social equality. But democracy is not just about freedom. Democracy, at its core, is about the *struggle* for freedom. The very shadow of freedom is slavery, defined by oppression in its variant forms, whether physical or spiritual. The democratic process is defined by an enantiodromia of violence to nonviolence, its cycle exemplifying the movement of invisible forces made manifest through humanity in its ongoing psychological and spiritual development.

The process of psychological, emotional and spiritual development, albeit individual or collective, is not linear. It is as unique as a fingerprint, with some patterns providing nodal points, small luminosities of consciousness emerging with each push in development, the pattern of light forming an interior underground railroad which the soul follows into life; its path of individuation.

This book is not a history book; however, highlighting periods of time which inform the collective development of the nation informs and contributes to the thesis. Therefore, this book will contain historical fact, psychological theory and the intersection between the two; the psycho-historical understanding of a specific period of development in American history. There will be references to the African American experience, utilizing the terms negro and black as well. These terms are not used as a smite to my fellow citizens. These terms are used in the context of history.

The American civil rights movement of the 1960s was followed by the women's liberation movement of the 1960s and 1970s. These undertakings, while having labor pains of their own, were preceded by bigger democratic earthquakes: The Emancipation Proclamation (passed January 1, 1863), the passing of the Thirteenth Amendment (January 31, 1865), and finally, the end of the Civil War (May 9, 1865). Each of these shifts was a response to the forces of oppression, originating within the individual, fueled by collective cultural forces. Cyclical oppression clouds the original point of a psychological split. Today, there is no greater evidence of America's national psychological split than in the political arena which is being energized by the complex of racism.

Since 2008, a race war resurfaced at the forefront of social and political movements in America. The election of Barack Obama brought a backlash from overt and covert facets of a racial complex endemic in the American psyche. Individuals may have denied their envy of a black man rising in the ranks of the political system, but blindness does not provide escape from the collective influence of this problem, for we have all inherited the complex, multifaceted problem of racism. To heal this cultural split, we must begin to share what we know about racism and how we experience it—otherwise, as with the protests of 2016 in the Charlottesville, Virginia, the split reappears in the guise of white supremacist groups marching with torches held aloft shouting, "Jews will not replace us!" while other groups march in opposition.

Just as White supremacy is but one facet of the cultural complex of racism, so is nonviolent integration of anti-racism. The utility of nonviolence as a spiritual weapon is an important transformational agent that induces order so that consciousness may arise within the complex.

How does change for the many occur from the individual? Although much has been written about the civil rights movement, little is understood about the psychological mechanisms that induce consciousness through nonviolent spiritual practice. Nonviolence reveals its pattern through event and circumstance, and with a common theme; its archaic, instinctual pattern is organized, powerful and purposeful. Through nonviolent implementation, the offender eventually reveals the true motive(s) behind his or her violent behavior.

The archetypal pattern of nonviolence is always implicitly present, its depth and breadth in a direct relationship to violence. While the civil rights movement of the 1950s and 1960s is in our national purview, a new era of civil rights is demanding a reckoning through the women's march on Washington of 2016, the "Me Too" movement of 2017–2018 and the immigration crisis of 2018. While physical and homicidal violence is historically on the decline globally, psychological violence from oppression and marginalization is on the rise in the United States and around the world (WGBH, 2019). The disease of despair is killing Americans at an alarming rate through suicide, alcohol and drug addiction (Moutier, 2019), not to mention institutionalized forms of racism.

In 2016 hate crimes in America were up for the second consecutive year, "with an uptick in incidents motivated by bias against Jews, Muslims, and LGBT people, among others, according to new FBI (Federal Bureau of Investigation) data" (Berman, 2017).

The FBI is alarmed at the increase in social unrest and the subsequent rise of hate crimes that the new political landscape has engendered in American life.

> Studies have shown increasing discrimination against Muslims in the United States. Jewish schools and institutions have been repeatedly shuttered by threats. Cities have struggled with how to handle white-supremacist groups seeking to hold rallies, and gay rights activists have decried what they describe as the Trump administration's 'all-out assault on LGBTQ people, women, and other minority communities.' The number of American hate groups also has increased, according to the Southern Poverty Law Center (Berman, 2017).

Governments and social structures and institutions traditionally provide the collective psychological guard rails and incentives for physical nonviolence as well as punishment(s) for violence. Yet, there are little to no social or psychological incentives which encourage the process of nonviolent consciousness outside of organized religion. As cultural and governmental institutions continue to fail in their responsibility to protect its citizens, the people who have been able to avoid the persecution of racism may soon find themselves vulnerable to the very hate crimes that have traditionally been inflicted upon the marginalized. The weakened moral fabric of institutional corruption has shifted the onus of consciousness from culture to the individual in order to preserve social order. With the moribund of religious institutions and corruption, many church followers have begun to abandon their religious affiliations in search of new spiritual containers. According to a Pew Research Center Poll:

> Between 2007 and 2014, the Christian share of the population fell from 78.4% to 70.6%, driven mainly by declines among mainline Protestants and Catholics. The unaffiliated experienced the most growth and the share of Americans who belonged to non-Christian faiths also increased. The widening gap of unaffiliated spiritual practitioners as well as an increasing number of agnostics (up from 16.1% to 22.8% in 2014), indicates that a growing number of Americans are suffering from a sense of spiritual alienation and existential angst. (Pew Research Center, 2015).

Our current national state of civil unrest is not just politically based. It reflects a deeper, moral and spiritual problem, the dissolution of the Monotheistic God image and subsequent focus on an ego-oriented existence. Nonviolent activism brings the practitioner face to face with their instinctual urge to power and aggression as well as the capacity to transform violence through a deeply connected experience with the other.

Nonviolence introduces the perpetrator to their own violent potential while instilling in the nonviolent practitioner an understanding of the other's deepest suffering. If the nonviolent demonstrator and perpetrator can withstand suffering together without acting violently, new compassion emerges, and a deeper understanding of a common humanity forms. The integration of shadow which emerges from nonviolence ignites the imagination giving birth to a dream.

The story of the march from Selma to Montgomery provides a window into our collective spiritual problem, and through nonviolent philosophy and its implementation, exemplifies how consciousness induces a change in the one and the many. The story begins with a nation in mourning and ends with a vision of hope during one of the nation's most bereft periods. The passing of the Voting Rights Act of 1965 reflects the healing of a split within the culture.

Chapter 1 explores the march from Selma to Montgomery, beginning on January 18, 1965, until the final walk into Montgomery on March 27, 1965. While each march cannot be depicted in detail, the reader will be introduced to the highlights of the march which lead to the passing of the Voting Rights Act of 1965. Key moments in the marches will include: the murder of Jimmie Lee Jackson and Reverend James Reeb, Bloody Sunday, Turnaround Tuesday, and the first and final days of the march across the bridge and into Montgomery, March 21, 1965.

Chapter 2 explores the phenomenon of the psychological complex; specifically focusing on the complex of racism, and its development within the individual and the culture. The projection-making factor within the complex and the development of the psychological split will be explored.

Chapter 3 introduces the reader to the lives of Mahatma Gandhi, Martin Luther King, Jr., and Carl Jung. The reader circumambulates their core values, how they were chosen by the collective as carriers of consciousness, as well as their contributions to nonviolent philosophy.

Chapter 4 focuses on the archetype of nonviolence, with its definition and amplification demonstrated through analytic case examples and events occurring during the marches in Selma. Gandhi's philosophical tenets of *Satyagraha* and *Ahimsa* and King's six tenets extracted from his book *Stride Toward Freedom* comprise the eightfold path of nonviolence.

Chapter 5 explores the archetypal experience of the march as the initiatory event of the individuation process and connects the one to the many through the psychological experience of the dream. The march and its symbolic significance will be unpacked through an exploration of the historical roots of marching in response to the forces of oppression being experienced both within the individual and culture.

Chapter 6 will focus on the archetype of the trickster and its role in the integration of shadow through nonviolent philosophy. The trickster tactics used in Selma were calculated, powerful and painful for they emerged from slave mythology. King's role as the archetypal trickster provided the essential alchemical ingredient necessary for change from the one to the many.

Chapter 7 focuses on the analytic interpretation of the march. The work of King, Jung and Gandhi's work will contribute to the analysis. The stages of the marches, the sacrifices, deaths, and attempts to cross the bridge illustrate the ego's attempt at confronting unconscious forces at work within the psyche which defends against a greater relationship with the archetypal Self.

Chapter 8 discusses the eightfold path of nonviolence and the implementation of the nonviolent tenets within the analytical hour. Each tenet will be defined, discussed and applied to C. G. Jung's Analytical Psychology through analytic case material.

Chapter 9 presents an analytic case through the implementation of nonviolent principles in analysis. Theories of transference and countertransference are explored as the effects of nonviolence unfold within the analytic experience.

Chapter 10 is a tribute to Dr. King's final book, *Where do we go from Here? Chaos to Community.* The chapter addresses the current and future question of racism in America, the cultural trauma that marginalization creates, as well as some nonviolent proposals for solutions to the problem. Moreover, *Where do we go From Here?* defines the current developmental crisis America is experiencing and where we might be heading.[1]

Note

1 The use of the term negro is utilized throughout this book, not as a smite or insult, but is being used within the historical context of the times within which the civil rights movement occurred.

References

Anderson, Devery S. (2015). *Emmett Till The Murder That Shocked the World and Propelled the Civil Rights Movement*, Jackson, University Press of Mississippi.

Berman, M. (2017, November 13). Hate crimes in the United States increased last year, the FBI says, *The Washington Post*. Retrieved from https://www.washingtonpost.com/news/post-nation/wp/2017/11/13/hate-crimes-in-the-united-states-increased-last-year-the-fbi-says/?utm_term=.5a48abfbf6a5.

King, M.L. (2014) *The Papers of Martin Luther King, Jr. Volume VII: To Save the Soul of America January 1961-August 1962*, Clayborn Carson (ed.) Oakland, University of California Press.

Pew Research Center. (2015, May 12) America's changing religious landscape, Pew Research Center. Retrieved from http://www.pewforum.org/2015/05/12/americas-changing-religious-landscape/.

Moutier, C. (2019, May 15). *The rate of suicides in the United States is growing – what can we do?* Retrieved from https://www.weforum.org: https://www.weforum.org/agenda/2019/05/the-global-suicide-rate-is-growing-what-can-we-do/.

WGBH (Director). (2019). *The Violence Paradox* [Motion Picture].

Chapter 1

The march from Selma to Montgomery
1965

January 2
Dr. King and leaders of the Southern Christian Leadership Conference are invited by Dallas County Voter's League, and Mrs. Amelia Boynton, to come to Selma to protest voting rights violations.

January 18
King leads a march to the Selma courthouse registrar's office to protest voting rights violations.

January 22
Teachers march takes place at the encouragement of F. D. Reese, an educator himself, who accompanies approximately 100 black teachers to the courthouse where the Superintendent and Jim Clark confront them.

January 23
Judge Daniel Harris issues a restraining order against Sheriff Clark and his attempts to keep potential voters away from the courthouse. An injunction grants at least 100 registrants at a time the right to stand in line at the courthouse to register.

January 25
Sheriff Clark assaults Annie Cooper, pushing her off the courthouse steps. She retaliates and assaults Sheriff Clark.

February 1
King jailed and Abernathy arrested.
Judge Thomas issues an injunction admonishing registrars for unfair tactics and imposes restrictions.

February 5
King Releases "A Letter from a Selma Jail" which is published in The New York Times.

February 18
A night march in Marion leads to the shooting of Jimmie Lee Jackson.

February 26
Jimmie Lee Jackson dies. James Bevel has synchronicity for the march from Selma to Montgomery while walking around outside of his motel, the "Torch Motel".

March 2
Memorial service held for Jimmie Lee Jackson in Marion, Alabama

March 7
Bloody Sunday

March 9
Turnaround Tuesday – Reverend James Reeb attacked in Selma after March; mortally wounded.

March 11
Reverend Reeb dies from brain injury.

March 15
Memorial services held at Browns Chapel for Reeb.

President Johnson delivers the speech, "The American Promise" calling to arms the conscience of a nation to fight against civil rights violations. He moves to pass the voting rights bill.

March 17
Federal Judge Frank Johnson grants movement the right to march from Selma to Montgomery.

March 21
March begins.

March 25
March ends on the steps of Capitol in Montgomery, with approximately 25,000 in attendance.

Viola Liuzzo murdered on her way back from Selma to Montgomery by members of the KKK.

August 6
President Johnson signs into law the Voting Rights Act of 1965.

The nonviolent civil rights movement began in the early 1900s when small factions of progressive and brave individuals rebelled against racism and violence. Ostensibly, organizations such as the Quakers and Mennonites hold nonviolence as a central tenet of practice. Religion provided the fulcrum for catapulting nonviolent theory into the social and political arenas. Such was the case for Martin Luther King's social-gospel ministry, which delivered nonviolent theory from the pulpit to the greater, collective civil rights movement.

According to Zunes and Laird (2010), in their article "The US Civil Rights Movement (1942–1968)," the 1940s marked a crucial nodal point in the development of civil rights, which began with the outlawing of legal segregation. Nonviolent action enlisted "litigation, the use of mass media, boycotts, demonstrations, as well as sit-ins and other forms of civil disobedience to turn public support against institutionalized racism and secure substantive reform in US law" (p. 12). These civil actions provided a crack in the persona of the American way of life, making way for the integration of shadow in the developmental crisis called civil rights.

Gandhian nonviolence had been introduced into the United States through organizations like the Fellowship of Reconciliation (FOR) and The Congress of Racial Equality (CORE), which began espousing the practice of nonviolence aimed at challenging the Jim Crow laws in the South. These progressive organizations were precursors of the civil rights movement (Zunes and Laird, 2010). With the seeds of nonviolent activism germinating throughout the Southern United States, American Blacks would finally be able to take advantage of the collective opening that World War II provided.

During World War II, America's diversity was greatly tested. The war effort relied on the labor of the suppressed African American female population while the men were primarily enlisted. Rosie the Riveter, Native American code talkers, and the Black aviators like the Tuskegee Airmen emerged to fortify the image of American strength. The minority thus became empowered during World War II. America's shadow had been awakened; the fight for freedom for the oppressed in Europe now had to be conducted on its own shores (Combs, 2014, pp. 3–7). While nonviolent activism coalesced in the 1940s, it was the murder of Emmett Till on August 28, 1955, that catalyzed the suppressed psychic contents of racism into the collective force of nature known as the civil rights movement. And while the movement's power was formed and carried by exceptionally talented, determined and courageous individuals within the collective, it would be one young man, whose ancestry, education and pedigree provided the necessary ingredients which set the stage to change the nation.

Looking back, it was all there, if one were to reflect upon it. Yet, many saw nothing particularly exceptional about the boy. King's life was designed to fit the times into which he was born. His childhood shaped his becoming and at the age of 25, this freshly minted Southern Baptist minister stepped into history when he founded the Montgomery Improvement Association (MIA), the organization which orchestrated the Montgomery Bus Boycotts 1955–1956. King's nomination and election as the President of the MIA set in motion what, until that moment in history, had been fits and starts of the civil rights movement.

Until 1965, the social and political environment in America in general, and in the South, in particular, had not changed much for the African American. Despite the passing of anti-segregation and civil rights legislation, the stranglehold of racism on the lives of negroes was evident in income disparity, poverty levels and voting numbers. Segments of white society were oppressing blacks by manipulating, coercing and denying them the right to vote through any means necessary. Nick Kotz, in his book *Judgment Days* (2005), reported that in 1965, Selma had only 1.9 percent of its qualified African American citizenship registered to vote (p. 255).

> As of April 1961, roughly 15,000 African Americans accounted for over 56 percent of the voting-age population in Selma and surrounding Dallas County, yet only 156 could vote. Despite tireless efforts to register voters—including constant litigation using the 1957, 1960, and 1964 Civil Rights Acts—only 355 blacks (2.1 percent) were registered to vote in Dallas County by late 1964 (pp. 255–256).

The system was supported by the state's Governor, George Wallace, as well as Colonel Al Lingo, the commander of Alabama's state troopers, and the Dallas County Judge James A. Hare, a staunch racist himself (pp. 256–257).

King always believed that if the negro couldn't vote, their world and the world at large would never change. Thus, King chose the small, dilapidated community of 27,000 (Kotz, 2005, p. 255) because it was the perfect crucible for the transformation of America's racist split. Selma had all the ingredients: a small Southern town that contained a corrupt political system and a minority white population whose racist aggression was only a hair's breadth away from exploding. And, lastly, King knew that Selma would capture the attention of the national press, the lens of consciousness from which the new collective psychic position would emerge.

From January 18 to March 25, 1965 King would lead many marches to the courthouse from the Brown's Chapel A.M.E. Church to the Dallas County Courthouse, where the demonstrators would confront the town's sheriff, James Clark. The marchers numbering in the hundreds would utilize non-violence tactics to trick the sheriff into a racist enactment, thus inciting aggression and sometimes physical violence. The enactment would then be captured via the nation's cameras and imminently broadcast on the nightly national news. The images captured the nation's attention, began a national dialogue about racism, and subsequently, led to passing of the Civil Rights Act of 1965. However, this process of nationally painful, tearing the scab of an old wound make conscious the gaping wound of racism within the American psyche. Thus, began the process of collective psychological movement of development.

In response to the marcher's endeavors, many institutionalized defenses were set in place to prevent the marches to the courthouse. Judges volleyed restraining orders and injunctions between the marchers and the town's officials as one side or the other bid to keep the marches going or quash the campaign's efforts altogether. Nevertheless, the demonstrations continued unabated.

The marches spread across Alabama and the nation, until finally, on February 18, 1965, a night march in Marion led to the death of Jimmie Lee Jackson, a black male who was beaten and shot by a police officer as Jimmie, and his grandfather sought refuge from the violence in a local cafe. From this tragedy, a synchronistic vision was born. Charles Fager, author of *Selma 1965* (1974), stated that Reverend James Bevel, a colleague of King's, had the idea to march to Montgomery while walking around outside of the "Torch Motel" (p. 81). The evening Bevel had the idea for the march, Jimmie Lee Jackson would die from his injuries.

Two days marked pivotal collective moments in the civil rights movement in particular and in Selma specifically; Bloody Sunday and Turn Around Tuesday. Bloody Sunday, March 7, became the first attempt to march to Montgomery from Selma. King was out of town for the first march; therefore, his colleague, John Lewis, head of Student Nonviolent Coordinating Committee (SNCC), headed the march, leading the group from the chapel to the Edmund Pettus Bridge. However, upon reaching the crest of the Edmund Pettus Bridge, the marchers were met by state troopers and law enforcement officials headed by Jim Clark. The marchers were verbally confronted, then physically attacked with whips and clubs, gassed, beaten, and forced back to the church. Upon regrouping, King and his lieutenants decided that it was time to bring together religious leaders from around the country to join them in their efforts to walk to Montgomery. Within a few days, thousands of spiritual leaders, politicians and activists had arrived in Selma to march with the demonstrators. Two days later, on Turn Around Tuesday, March 9, 1965, the few that began the movement had multiplied by the tens of thousands across the country, as other cities also held demonstrations.

On the second day of the official march to Selma, King, along with over 2,500 marchers, found themselves standing in the eye of the storm filled with a singular purpose. President Johnson, fearing more deaths and violence in Selma, issued a federal injunction forbidding King to march. According to David Garrow, author of *Bearing the Cross* (1986), King, feeling pressured to defy the government, became entangled in a moral dilemma that would pull him from all sides (p. 402).

Johnson asked that King avoid more violence by delaying the march to Montgomery. King refused. Johnson sent his top aide, LeRoy Collins, to

Selma to negotiate with King. He vowed a nonviolent response from law enforcement if King and the marchers would turn around on the bridge. King again refused. In a last-ditch effort, Collins negotiated a deal with the law enforcement waiting on the opposite side of the bridge. They vowed that if King turned around on the bridge, they would not harm the marchers. According to several sources, King's trickster-like response to Johnson's plea via Collins were varied. "Some say his response (to Collins) was non-committal—perhaps a simple smile" (Garrow, 1978, p. 88). Fager stated "There is uncertainty as to whether Dr. King explicitly agreed to go along with this plan or not, but it appears that he did" (1974, p. 102). King stated he would turn around on the bridge but he could not guarantee that his people would follow. (Kotz, 2005, p. 294).

King, flanked by high-ranking officials in the Southern Christian Leadership Conference, the SNCC, and religious leaders from around the country began the second attempt to march to Montgomery on Tuesday, March 9. Upon reaching the far side of the Edmund Pettus, the marchers faced a sea of blue state troopers blocking their way. King halted in front of the troopers and, after singing "We Shall Overcome," asked if he and others could kneel and pray. A brief silence passed. King rose from his knees and then turned around to lead the group back to the church. Just as they turned, however, the line of troopers that had been blocking the highway suddenly withdrew to the side of the road leaving it wide open. Indeed, "If there was a secret script for the confrontation, the state then violated the agreement" because the state had forbidden King to march (Fager, 1974, p. 104).

The evening of Turnaround Tuesday, Americans were once again made aware of the volatile cocktail of racism sitting at the core of the civil rights movement when Reverend James Reeb was savagely attacked by a group of white racists and died from his injuries a few days later. The country's outrage forced Johnson into alignment with King and a desire to end the violence through the immediate passing of legislation. Speaking to the nation about the mortal wound of America's racism, President Johnson stated:

> At times history and fate meet at a single time in a single place to shape a turning point in man's unending search for freedom. So it was at Lexington and Concord. So it was a century ago at Appomattox. So it was last week in Selma, Alabama (The History Place, 1965).

Johnson's speech unified the political and moral landscapes of the nation leading to the march from Selma to take place six days later.

"Fifty-four miles—a total of 285,120 feet walked over the course of five days" defined the distance which led to the steps of Montgomery and the passing of the Voting Rights Act of 1965, five months later (Combs, 2014, p. 110). On March 21, 1965, 8,000 marchers set off from Brown's Chapel and for the third and final time, crossed over the Edmund Pettus Bridge and walked for the next five days. The demonstrators arrived in Montgomery on March 25, 1965, with tens of thousands of people gathered in Montgomery, who had come to greet the marchers. What had begun in 1955 with Emmett Till and Rosa Parks would end on the steps of the capital culminating with King's powerful speech, culminating in a partial recitation of Samuel Francis Smith's lyrics to "My Country 'Tis of Thee."

References

Combs, B. H. (2014). *From Selma to Montgomery: The Long March to Freedom*. New York: Routledge.

Fager, C. (1974). *Selma 1965: The March that Changed the South*. New York: Charles Schribner's and Sons.

Garrow, D. (1986). *Bearing the Cross*. New York: Perennial Classics.

Garrow, David (1978). *Protest at Selma Martin Luther King, Jr. and the Voting Rights Act of 1965*. Binghamton, The Vail-Ballou Press.

Kotz, N. (2005). *Judgment Days*. Boston: Houghton Mifflin Company.

The History Place (1965). We Shall Overcome. Retrieved fromwww.historyplace.com/speeches/johnson.

Zunes, Stephen and Laird, J. (2010, January). The US Civil Rights Movement (1942–1968). Retrieved from https://www.nonviolent-conflict.org:https://www.nonviolent-conflict.org/us-civil-rights-movement-1942-1968/.

Chapter 2

The complex of racism

It is Monday, March 1, 1965, one day after the memorial service for Jimmie Lee Jackson, the first victim of the Selma movement. It is also voting registration day, the nodal point from which a new movement across the nation had begun one month earlier when Marin Luther King, Jr. and company had arrived in the dilapidated town of Selma to conduct a voting rights campaign. King leaves Selma checkerboarding across the back roads of Alabama, stopping at strategic voting registration offices to have meet and greets with supporters as well as confrontations with those officials who stood in the way of voting registration for blacks. On his way through Lowndes County, King stopped in the small town of Hayneville, where he found himself in a faceoff with the town's voting registrar, Carl Golson. Golson had just tricked black registrants into marching to the town's jail to register. The demonstrators returned to the courthouse only to be told by Golson that registration was closed. The demonstrators, soaked from the rain, and fatigued by the wild goose chase, turned to King for support (Fager, 1974, pp. 82–84).

King confronts the angry registrar who tells him that he's not welcome to register if he isn't from Lowndes County. King states, "We don't understand." The registrar, his authority challenged retorts, "You are damned dumb then if you don't understand." King leans into the moment, nonviolently confronting the registrar and asks, "Are you a Christian?" The registrar responds, "Yes, I'm a Methodist, but what has Christianity to do with the vote?" (Fager, 1974, p. 84).

There is disunion in the answer that the voting registrar gives to Dr. King. Yet, King, known for his tenacity and courage does not back down, for his penetrating question lays bare the central moral problem in America. His gift of sword-bearing consciousness was painfully wielded on the nation at large during the civil rights movement and was swiftly brought to bear in his question to the registrar. In the very nature of the question, King penetrates to the heart of racism in the South and the psychological split which defined the hypocrisy in Golson's attitude. Unfortunately, the registrar misses the moment, clearly not comprehending the truth that the nonviolent confrontation aims to uncover. He turns away from his conscience and instead relies upon a set of beliefs about race constructed of longstanding patterns of ideas, images, memories, dreams and affects; an intricate yet sturdy psychic system which culturally and personally defines him.

The registrar is caught within a web of deceit purchased by his ego and enforced by his surroundings, which provide him with a lifestyle free from psychological and moral scrutiny. Indeed, the registrar does not see that his way of life is destructive to other human beings. Any awareness of hypocrisy is outweighed by a confluence of factors involving personal, economic, cultural and collective beliefs about power and race. He cannot acknowledge the moral infraction being committed in his racist actions because he is caught in the grip of the racial complex. The complex engulfs his ego to such a degree that any awareness of wrongdoing, remains unconscious, and if the registrar is conscious of wrongdoing, the infraction is defended by his ego. His ego only relates to what he sees and knows in his immediate, Southern experience as a white male, historically affected and defined by the trauma of racism. Similarly, King is a Southern black male who carries the trauma of racism in a very different way. Both men carry the cultural split, with each side defined by the archetypal master–slave paradigm: one side opposing the other, joined but separated by the trauma. The entire American problem of racism is captured in a moment in time, setting both men on edge, one holding an active non-violent stand openly challenging the status quo, while the other is emotionally activated, openly hostile, asserting dominance, and challenging King's intellect, intent and rightful assertion of power.

What is this force of nature that commands a man so powerfully that he is willing to gamble his livelihood, family and maybe even his own life? King's work revolved around the disunion between the American ideals of freedom and equality espoused by the Constitution and the falsities of that promise; particularly in the lives of African Americans. He addressed the complex of racism in the American psyche and worked tirelessly to attain rights for African Americans through nonviolent activism.

The phenomenon of the psychological complex is known to have originated from the work of French Psychologist Pierre Janet (Ellenberger, 1970, p. 406). Depth Psychologist Eugen Bleuler also contributed to the theory of the complex (Jacobi, 1959, p. 6). However, it was Carl Gustav Jung, a Swiss Psychiatrist, and founder of the school of Analytical Psychology, who emphasized the role of complexes in psychological life. Jung's complex theory was the original name given to his analytic school of thought. From complex theory, Jung developed the word-association test enabling its practitioner to locate within the examinee areas of psychological duress, which would indicate the existence of a psychological complex. The word-association test became the forerunner of the modern polygraph test.

The main feature of a complex is affect. The complex itself can be thought of as emotionally charged psychic experiences consisting of memories, dreams, thoughts or fantasies around a specific topic; for instance, mother, father, work, religion, etc. According to Jung,

> Every molecule [of the complex] participates in this feeling tone, so that, whether it appears by itself or in conjunction with others, it always carries this feeling tone with it, and it does this with the greater distinctness the more we can see its connection with the complex-situation as a whole (Jacobi, 1959, p. 8).

Complexes are powerful experiences which, in totality, comprise much of our inner psychological world. Whether individual or cultural, Jung (1960) stated that we need our complexes, because they hold our world together, while at the same time posing personal difficulties (para. 142–143). The word-association test enables the psychologist to conceptualize a patient's world view as well as to understand which complexes hold powerful sway in the patient's psyche. Jung's development of the association test was pioneering due to its capacity to scientifically measure unconscious phenomena, thus legitimizing the unconscious as the other half of the psychological life. Had the registrar been subjected to the word-association test, his results would have pointed to a highly activated psychic experience around any words associated with race.

When one is caught in the net of a complex, it can feel as if one is not in charge of themselves. Complexes show themselves in a myriad of ways, for instance, through compulsive giggling, forgetfulness or slips of the tongue. Complexes can also bring tremendous tornadic affect, defined by trauma and archetypal possession; such as in racial hatred, or political divisiveness.

A constellated complex indicates that the person's unconscious mind has drawn together psychological elements, which can then take over disturbing one's state of consciousness. Jung described complexes as, little internal "devils" that

> seem to delight in playing impish tricks. They slip just the wrong word into one's mouth, they make one forget the name of the person one is about to introduce, they cause a tickle in back of the throat just when the softest passage is being played on the piano at a concert, they make the tiptoeing latecomer trip over a chair with a resounding crash (Jung, 1960, para. 202).

For example, in a television interview, Selma's mayor, Joseph Smitherman suffers from a slip-of-the-tongue when discussing the effect the marches are having on Selma:

> Our city (Selma) and our country have been subjected to the greatest pressures. I think any community in this country's had to withstand. We've had in our area here outsider agitation groups of all levels. We've had Martin Luther 'coon;' pardon, I mean Martin Luther King.... (DeVinney, 1987, 6:00).

The mayor's need for self-correction demonstrates the complex at work within an arena of highly charged feelings around racism. The complex's power spills over into consciousness, despite the mayor's attempts to defend the actions of the city's law enforcement officials. His need to defend his community from "outside agitation groups," reveals the cultural complex at work in the South in particular, as well as the challenge that the demonstrators posed to the integrity of the complex.

When complexes begin to surface, it is a compelling experience defined by overwhelming affect and a patterned response as unique as a fingerprint, containing familial, ancestral and cultural roots. The racial complex that emerges from the experience of oppression and an abuse of power does not diminish over time until and unless a galvanic reading on the moral scale within the individual causes a seismic shift in one's conscience. Yet, an individual like Golson, who is of a Southern identity carries with him an ego-syntonic perspective of racism, where his internal and cultural values are aligned with his, making his ego and its attitude to the conscious world one and the same. His ego and outer world define the reality he believes to be moral and just. It may very well be that the only problem he sees with race is in the African American's desire to stir up the status quo. In order for Golson to develop the capacity to expand the depth and breadth of his conscience, he would need to develop a relationship with his unconscious world where his complexes reside and begin to uncover the hypocrisy in his one-sided position on race.

Complexes are complicated because they inform perception, affecting positive or negative projections. Projections are the transference of subjective experiences onto the other. Negative projections consist of shadow elements unknown to ego consciousness contributing to the creation of potential violence. For example, the registrar's projection that King was "damned dumb" may well be the registrar's unowned insecurities.

Intense collective emotion is the hallmark of an activated cultural complex at the core of which is an archetypal pattern. Cultural complexes structure emotional experience and operate in the personal and collective psyche in much the same way as individual complexes, although their content might be quite different. Like individual complexes, cultural complexes tend to be repetitive, autonomous, resist consciousness, and collective experience that confirms their historical point of view (Kimbles and Singer, 2004, p. 6). As the civil rights movement aptly demonstrated the intersection of personal and cultural complexes can be psychological food for tremendous cultural upheaval, turbulence and potential violence.

Jung's greatest contribution to the field of psychology consists of the idea that we are all connected uniquely through a universal language revealed through affectively based psychic patterns known as *archetypes*. Archetypes contain the unique experience of the individual, but also hold psychic experiences and images shared by all human beings since the beginning of time, and these experiences share a commonality, a behavioral and spiritual DNA, if you will. For example, motherhood is an intimate personal experience for every mother, and yet, her motherhood is also deeply connected to a vast storehouse of human experiences of motherhood. In this way, a mother carries an instinctual knowledge of mothering throughout the ages in her capacity to give birth and raise her offspring. Archetypes are bi-polar in nature and thus move between instinctual, biologically based experiences, up into the spiritual realm of human existence.

The archetypal experience of the master–slave constitutes a large portion of America's national shadow, which is defined by the instinctual urge to power through physical ownership of the other according to skin color, religion, etc., to spiritual possession, or dominance over the other. Consciousness, or one's capacity to integrate shadow through the inner relatedness between one's ego and one's self, weakens the negative master–slave, and thus introduces the positive master–slave, or self to ego relationship.

Oppression or the urge to power permeates the complex from its outer edges to its epicenter. At the center of the complex is the archetype of the master–slave, humankind's original split, the archetypal pattern that is endlessly expressed through the complex. Perception draws energy to the archetype and through a myriad of psychological and emotional factors, constellates the complex. Indeed, a complex can be tornadic in nature destroying everything in its wake. Jung stated, "Only when you have seen whole families destroyed by them morally and physically, and the unexampled tragedy and hopeless misery that follow in their train, do you feel the full impact of the reality of complexes" (1960, para. 209).

Among the primary affective experiences of the racialized complex are voicelessness, silence, fear of annihilation, abuse of power, hatred, and blindness. Voicelessness consumes the deepest part of the complex, which contributes to and robs the victim of their due process. Like abuse of any kind, the perpetrator binds the victim forever to their breast through the silence; a pact created at the boundary crossing of the initial violation.

The freest among us to speak of racism at its rawest and most honest level are the children. For children have not yet been fully conditioned by the complex. They are immersed in the closest realm to the truth, the unconscious, where consciousness lies in wait to be discovered through their eyes. And, they have a habit of discovering the truth at the uncanniest of times, especially when adults are the most vulnerable and unprepared for their honesty.

Ben, aged seventy-five, still recalls with pain and shame the first time he confronted his parents about the racism that surrounded him, defining his seven-year-old life. For a child, love is not segregated, or marked by vectors such as skin color. Growing up in rural Mississippi, Ben recalls his true home being the town's general store, which his parents owned and operated most of his life. As he reflects on his childhood and his lifelong struggle with understanding racism, he unfurls his experiences with a commanding immediacy.

The purity of his innocence had not yet been tarnished by time corrupting his razor-sharp moral compass. The young Ben needs answers to this racism quagmire, and more, especially since someone he deeply loves is caught in this puzzling riddle. Perhaps this is Ben's first betrayal, his first heartbreak following an experience of a love which shows no discrimination, but instead loyalty, devotion and timeless syncopation with his own soul's rhythms. Will, known as an African American "hand" in the Deep South during Ben's childhood years, is an important and integral part of the family. He assists in anything the family needs to run the orderliness of their daily lives. He raises Ben in every practical sense of the word; teaches him manners, morals, common sense, and from time to time mischievous brotherly antics, imbuing Ben's life with a sense of love, humor and purpose not since forgotten.

Will's powerful presence could be confusing for Ben, because while he is such a seminal force in young Ben's life, Will is forced to conduct himself away from the family in ways that Ben doesn't quite understand, for example, eating his dinner all alone on the porch just off the kitchen. This arrangement leaves Ben feeling uncomfortable and confused. This obvious moral fracture in the fabric of Ben's world is defined by a general dis-ease around the dinner table, an edgy silence. On the afternoon Ben decides to crack the code of this highly disquieting inner experience, he finds himself at a crossroads between his curiosity and the silent rules that define his young life. From the dinner table, he can see Will take his usual seat, just outside his purview. Who knows what breaks the moment of stalemate in the silence of a complex, but Ben's little mind can no longer tolerate the confusion. He decides to ask his parents the forbidden question, "Why doesn't Will have dinner with us?" While the barrier of silence that defines the complex has been briefly penetrated by Ben's question, he can feel for the first time, the slamming of an inner door, forbidding him access. In the steely silence he experiences from his parents, Ben knows that he is not going to get an answer.

Ben persists in his determination to understand this breach of love's goodness, indeed because of his love for Will, and because he is convinced that if his parents won't give him the answer, Will certainly would. So, off to the porch, he marches, "Will, why don't you eat dinner with us?" Again, Ben's question is met with silence. Will, being a man of wisdom and common sense, probably knows to tread lightly, for the silence in the complex has him firmly by the throat as well. Caught in a moment of crisis with his own conscience, Will looks down at his plate, and then out into the distance, clearly attempting to formulate a safe enough response, he answers quietly, "Well, I like it just fine here where I am." The thud of betrayal must have been difficult to hold. Perhaps Ben's parents, and Will, were attempting to shield Ben from racism and its ugly truths. Maybe they thought Ben did not need to know of such inequities because he would not understand. But racism was known to Ben without it having to be discussed or taught. Through the viaducts of the unconscious and his life in the South in particular, Ben became a recipient of the complex. In the asking of the question, the stony silence became the entry point of the infection. Lest the world around him crumble, the dictum "We do not talk openly about racism" had to be upheld. In this communal delusion of blindness and silence, Ben made a choice. In doing so, he realized that at that moment, everyone he trusted had lied to him, and this truth sits with him now, seventy years later.

Sitting at the core of the complex of racism is the power instinct; the desire to control the other through an absolute negation of the other's need through psychological ownership. How this abuse of power is inflicted upon the other is determined by the psychic makeup of the perpetrator, the victim, and the cultural values and expectations of the environment. Indeed, the complexes of the individual can intersect with the complexes of the culture creating a cavalcade of emotional turmoil. In the face of a cultural complex an individual may become completely immersed within the history of a community, and the events that define the culture to such a degree that the individual ego becomes subsumed in the face of the cultural complex, because the individual and the cultural complexes may suffer from similar traumas.

According to Thomas Singer and Catherine Kaplinsky in the book entitled *Jungian Analysis* (2010), "Cultural complexes can be defined as emotionally charged aggregates of ideas and images that tend to cluster around an archetypal core and are shared by individuals within an identified collective" (p. 5). Furthermore, Thomas Singer and Samuel Kimbles, editors of *The Cultural Complex: Contemporary Jungian Perspectives on Psyche and Society* state that:

> "Cultural complexes can be thought of arising out the cultural unconscious as it interacts with both the archetypal and personal realms of the psyche and the broader outer world arena of schools, communities, media and all the other forms of cultural and group life. As such, cultural complexes can be thought of as forming the essential components of an inner sociology (2004, p. 4).

The building blocks of the South's inner sociology act like a psychic skin, an invisible psychic container which enables both sides of the racial split to live accordingly separate but together, as the complex dictates. Yet, the split keeps the souls of the individuals within the split holistically separated from themselves and each other, divided by history and defined by fear.

For example, in 2013, I traveled back to Alabama, to the small town in which I was raised. I was struck by the power of the racialized complex, still viscerally alive, some fifty-two years later. Driving from Birmingham to the southernmost tip of the state I noticed that not much had changed; the town I grew up in seemingly barely affected by the passing of time, the signs of modernity invisible to the roaming eye. Buildings leaned cockeyed with paint peeling like shedding skin, while old antebellum houses belonging to the

town's established white citizenry remained ageless, looking as they had decades earlier, polished, standing proud, holding court, only the streets showing
signs of aging. I had the same uncanny feeling earlier in the day while
traveling through Selma.

As memories unpeel one street at a time, I find myself sitting in front of a
favorite family restaurant, still standing after fifty years, which specializes in
the fried Southern cuisine I delighted in as a small child: fried catfish and
hushpuppies, black-eyed peas and cornbread, stewed green beans, and berry
cobbler. An African American man stands outside the back of the restaurant
smoking a cigarette when I drive up. As if on cue the young man looks up at
me and my car, quickly surmising that I am not a regular. The rhythm of life
in the South is greatly disturbed by outsiders; indeed, the stasis that overlays
small southern towns is palpable and at times ominous.

"Can I help you?" he says with a wide grin. I smile and respond in kind. As
he confirms the location of the restaurant, he also tells me that he is the cook,
and invites me in. The cement floors, vinyl dining chairs and walled photo-
graphs layered with grease line the walls. As in a small-town way, all heads
turn when I walk in. After being seated with a plateful of food from the
buffet, the cook emerges from the kitchen and takes a seat at my table. It
doesn't take long before I begin to vibrate with a mild indiscernible anxiety,
which I dismiss as a mild excitement. I notice a group of white-haired,
Southern men in the back of the restaurant, sitting in closed quarters talking
in low murmurs, coughs and guttural sputters which form the fits and starts
of conversation which I imagine revolves around local gossip.

As the cook begins a congenial conversation with me, I discern a stirring in
my stomach, and a buzz in my ears, as the sudden silence from the tables
around me becomes apparent. The air develops a thick valence of heat and
moisture loaded with a feeling of dread. Something begins to give way inside
of me, but the cook doesn't seem to notice. It is the same sensation one
experiences in a quiet that precedes an earthquake. An awareness that something is beginning to seismically shift settles into my stomach. I look down
and around to see if anyone else is preparing for the jolt. The clanging of
everyone else's dishes has ceased as the scaffolding creaks. The sense of sta-
bility I look for within myself isn't there. My disorientation causes me to lose
my appetite. The disturbing cultural neurosis forms in my wooden, brittle
smile as I attempt to convey that I'm enjoying the conversation and the food,
which I can no longer taste.

The walls begin to feel as if they have eyes, and my back senses that it is
being deeply penetrated by the glares of the white men who are now sitting in
silence. The constructs of time and space slip away as fear envelopes me. I
know the rage of the white man in a different way than the cook does, the
outcome of which may mean death for him, shame, humiliation and aliena-
tion for me. My fear compels me to flee. I begin looking for the exit—both
from the conversation and the building. He smiles and leans in, "So, what

brings you to Alabama from Phoenix?" I smile, but I'm certain it appears more like a grimace around the edges. I wipe my mouth with my napkin but want to shove it inside to stifle my silent scream. I want to yell, "Stop talking to me before you get lynched!" I long to continue our conversation, but an age-old barrier slams the door shut. Something historic and threatening disrupts our intended harmony. I am caught not just in my own personal fear but within something alive in the culture, perhaps even within the soil itself. It is more than my individual history, for it is loaded with the mythological underpinnings of the greater South. My eyes drift up and behind him to the exit and the cash register where the white owner is glaring at me. I begin calculating how long it will take me to get to my car. I thank him for the meal, which I'm angry I can no longer taste, pay my bill in haste and flee.

Sitting in my car I sit emotionally spinning in the complex, staring out the windshield wondering to myself what in the hell just happened. While it has been more than half a century since I left the state of Alabama, it feels as if time has not shifted the paradigm at all.

Psychologically I carry some inner affective, emotional, and psychic image of the racial complex which is palpable and emotionally dysregulating. In a split moment in time, I am entwined and entrapped in a timeless experience filled with guilt and shame.

I begin to wonder what I would have really done had the situation drastically changed had he been threatened by the men inside the restaurant. Would I defend him or flee? The paralysis I am experiencing informs me of the terror within the complex. Indeed, within a constellated complex, feeling takes over making reflective consciousness exceedingly difficult.

James Baldwin aptly stated that racism is a cultural phenomenon that can be justified when having to make a Faustian bargain with oneself between losing everything one knows as a sense of security.

> Men who knew that slavery was wrong were forced, nevertheless, to fight to perpetuate it because they were unable to turn against 'blood and kin and home.' And when blood and kin and home were defeated, they found themselves, more than ever, committed: committed, in effect, to a way of life which was unjust and crippling as it was inescapable (Baldwin, 1985, p. 106).

Perhaps the voting registrar of Hayneville was defending his way of life, deeply threatened by the idea of inner change. His ego had been traditionally defined by loyalty to one side of the split; a loyalty which might greatly sacrifice his sense of autonomy should he empathize with the other side. Furthermore, in this loyalty to blood, kin and home, he denies the black man those same rights by refusing him the right of voter registration.

Racism is defined by a particular kind of hatred. Hate shines out from the complex of racism as a primary affective experience. Hate hides in the folds of fundamentalism and is difficult to dissolve, if at all. Hate is formed of a kind of hubris that can paralyze the ego, making shared likeness, difficult to integrate into one's humanity. In *Stride Towards Freedom*, King stated: "Men often hate each other because they fear each other; they fear each other because they do not know each other, they do not know each other because they cannot communicate; they do not communicate because they are separated" (1958, p. 33).

Racism is a shared wound in our American narrative, which is not going away, each of us playing a part in the master–slave archetypal relationship system. Our history defines the racial privileged not by economic wealth, but by skin color. And as Baldwin stated, "Havens are high priced. The price exacted of the haven dweller is that he contrives to delude himself into believing that he has found a haven" (Baldwin, 1985, p. 12). Statistics from the US Census Bureau predict that by 2042, the white population in America will be in the minority. The dominance of non-Hispanic white people, who today account for two-thirds of Americans, will be whittled away, falling steadily to less than half in 2042 and to 46 percent by 2050. In the opposite trajectory, those who describe themselves as Hispanic, African American, Asian and Native American will increase in proportion from about a third now to 54 percent by 2050 (Pilkington, 2008).

In a new Brookings Institute report (Frey, 2018), the white population will become the minority sooner than expected as the new statistics reveal that the "nation will become 'minority white' in 2045. During that year, whites will comprise 49.9 percent of the population in contrast to 24.6 percent for Hispanics, 13.1 percent for blacks, 7.8 percent for Asians, and 3.8 percent for multiracial populations." As the scales begin to tip over into a paradigm of historical opposites where whites become the minority, Americans are already grappling with the newly diverse ethnic and racial paradigm. Our bloody national history on racism provides the clues to what will happen economically and socio-politically as the landscape of America's racial divide dramatically changes. The question remains to be answered as to how we will manage the inevitable upheaval of aggression and violence as the consequent agents of change swing into action.

Racism was an enigma to me as a child. I did not understand racist hatred and all of its ugly permutations until I witnessed Dr. King through the grainy images of my television set. Dr. King and his civil rights colleagues formed a new paradigm around the objectification of the American negro, humanizing their suffering. Through the images of the civil rights movement, the missing pieces in the riddle began to form into a language I could understand. He made sense of an insanity taking place that no one on my side of town was willing to talk about. Finally, all the questions I held in my mind made sense to me, but why whites hated blacks was as illogical to me as the Vietnam war was; a war my father had been sent off to fight, two times over. It was Dr. King who introduced me to the shadow side of the South in the 1960s; an expected loyalty to family, community and white politics, a white superiority often disguised within the folds of southern gentility, generosity and charm. Indeed, Dr. King put into words what defined the real split between blacks and whites. In this murky area between the Southern persona and Southern history, Dr. King's nonviolence revealed the ugly truth about America's great national shadow. Indeed, it seemed that violence defined my childhood, something Dr. King helped me to put into perspective. Today, I believe that it was King's compassion, love, and refusal to hate that allowed for an agapeic form of divine love to enter into my being soothing my very real childhood depression, providing me with a sense of hope. The hope emerged from an understanding deep within me, created by the witnessing of the civil rights movement through my television set. Somehow in the midst of it all, I believe my ego was able to grasp that what I had been intuiting was right, that racism and war were wrong. It was not that my parents had not talked with me about the immorality of racism, it was the contradictions that existed between my family and community that confused me. We pledged allegiance in school, while cheering for the re-election of our segregationist Governor, while being told by my parents that racism was wrong.

In the cultural complex my ego could not grasp that there was a world outside of the racialized complex, the complex and I were one. My ego-syntonic attitude occluded any shadow knowledge. Yet, intuitively, I knew something wasn't right. According to Kimbles and Singer:

> Intense collective emotion is the hallmark of an activated cultural complex at the core of which is an archetypal pattern. Cultural complexes structure emotional experience and operate in the personal and collective psyche in much the same way as individual complexes, although their content might be quite different. Like individual complexes, cultural complexes tend to be repetitive, autonomous, resist consciousness, and collect experience that confirms their historical point of view (2004, p. 6).

In his article entitled, "Racism: Processes of Detachment, Dehumanization, and Hatred," psychoanalyst Farhad Dalal, describes how we can become psychosocially conditioned to racism. These psychosocial structures underpin the cultural complex which informs our individual development and complexes, thus conditioning the personality to identify with racism as a real phenomenon.

> The fact that we inhabit a racialized and color-coded world means that, through the psychosocial developmental process, each of us, of necessity, imbibes a version of that world order, such that our psyches, too, become more color coded and racialized. And then, in turn, we continue to reproduce and sustain the processes of racialization, despite our efforts not to do so (2006, p. 156).

The racial divide sits at the center of one of America's greatest shadow complexes. While complexes are autonomous and never truly resolved, it is in the union of the split sides, no matter how brief, that healing can occur. It is through a relationship of commonality that the divide might close. Bridging can occur through nonviolent activism, which holds the split sides in a creative tension of relationship while a third, new way emerges. Selma demonstrated this process in action.

References

Baldwin, J. (1985). *The Evidence of Things Not Seen*. New York: Henry Holt.

Dalal, Farhad (2006). Racism: Processes of Detachment, Dehumanization and Hatred. *The Psychoanalytic Quarterly*, 75(1): 131–161.

DeVinney, C. C. (Director). (1987). *Eyes on the Prize, Part 6: The Bridge to Freedom* [Motion Picture].

Ellenberger, H. F. (1970). *The Discovery Of The Unconscious*. New York: Basic Books, Inc.

Fager, C. E. (1974). *Selma 1965: The March That Changed The South*. (C. S. Sons, ed.) New York: Berne Convention.

Frey, W. H. (2018, March 14). The US will become 'minority white' in 2045: Youthful minorities are the engine of future growth. Retrieved from https://www.brookings.edu/blog/the-avenue/2018/03/14/the-us-will-become-minority-white-in-2045-census-projects/.

Jacobi, J. (1959). *Complex Archetype Symbol*. Princeton: Princeton University Press.

Jung, C. (1960). *The Collected Works of C.G. Jung, Volume 8. The Structure and Dynamics of Psyche*. Princeton: Princeton University Press.

Kimbles, Samuel and Singer, Thomas (2004). *The Cultural Complex: Contemporary Jungian Perspectives on Psyche and Society*. London, New York: Routledge.

King, Jr. Martin Luther (1958). *Stride Toward Freedom: The Montgomery Story*. Boston: Beacon Press.

Pilkington, E. (2008, August 14). *US set for dramatic change as white America becomes minority by 2042*. Retrieved from *The Guardian*: https://www.theguardian.com/world/2008/aug/15/population.race.

Singer, Thomas and Kaplinsky, Catherine (2010). Murry Stein (ed), "Cultural Complexes in Analysis" in *Jungian Psychoanalysis: Working in the Spirit of C.G. Jung*. Chicago, La Salle: Open Court.

Chapter 3

Gandhi, King, and Jung

Mahatma Gandhi, Martin Luther King, Jr., and Carl Jung were revolution-aries during their lifetimes, procuring their own philosophical approaches to life in their quest for spiritual truth. These three leaders would change the world with their theories of soul, urging humanity to attend to the violent aspects of personality through the cultivation of a conscious life. In sum, their work returns the onus of humans' responsibility for the proliferation of evil onto the individual and, through the individual's inner transformation, affect change for the greater good.

Gandhi's nonviolent activism focused on the Hindu concepts of *Satyagraha* and *Ahimsa*. *Satyagraha* is the active pursuit of the truth or consciousness in the face of violence. The Satyagrahi's refusal to allow violence forces into consciousness the truth of what is being suppressed. Consequently, inflictors of violence experience the suffering beneath the aggression are brought into an awareness of their behavior, and thus exposed to their full humanity.

Ahimsa is one's dedication to a nonviolent life in thought, word, and deed. The conscious cultivation of *Ahimsa* is ultimately a feminine practice of psychological holding, marked by an emotional stance of openness and receptivity. The implementation of *Satyagraha* and *Ahimsa* unconsciously creates psychological boundaries around which violent urgings can be contained and alchemically transformed.

Fabrizio Petri (2014), in his article "Gandhi, Jung and Nonviolence Today," compared the concepts of Gandhi's *Ahimsa* and Jung's *Anima*, referring to them as feminine practices. *Anima* cultivation occurs through one's access to the unconscious, an essential bridge in the individuation process. According to Petri, Jung (1939) inferred that,

> to become oneself means for the ego to deal with the unconscious since the latter is the source of the renewal of the human psyche and, therefore, human personality. "The autonomy of the unconscious begins where emotions are borne," said Jung, and "Anima is the unavoidable medium—an energy converter of sorts—to such an experience." (p. 10)

For Petri, *Ahimsa*, and *Anima* are similar concepts (pp. 10–11). The cultivation of *Ahimsa* and *Anima* can lead to what King frequently espoused as *Agape*, or divine love, a collective unifier.

Kingian nonviolence made the process of shadow integration possible by projecting the cultural trauma of racism onto the national stage via the media and effecting societal change by drawing the sociopolitical forces of the nation into a dialog for change. Although King's nonviolent movement primarily addressed racism, his acumen as a minister and activist appealed to the masses, gifting King the national pulpit to speak on the moral problems America faced with racism, poverty, and militarism. King was the embodiment of the American problem and solution to racism, making him the most effective channel for the Self's manifestation in culture.

Jungian psychology focuses on shadow integration, and with the individuation process taking shadow integration one step further. The final phase of individuation involves the ego's surrender to the self, a mysterious process altogether, for it involves a leap of faith into an instinctively sensed, but essentially unknown realm of existence. For Jung, the unconscious world contains shadow material as well as a reservoir of life force energy that, when plumbed through dream, myth, or imagination, can lead to a significant existential experience. Labeled by Jung as the collective unconscious, this vast storehouse of human experience lies below the threshold of the personal unconscious. When accessed, it can mediate one's destructive instinctual urges to power and aggression and connect one to the collective, thereby imbuing the personality with a sense of purpose and meaning. Having consistent access to one's unconscious life is therefore crucial to psychological health. Jung's study of the archetypal Self became the thrust of his work and his greatest contribution to psychology.

Gandhi, King, and Jung influenced history; their legacies driven by a common purpose: the procurement of psychological wholeness through the development of a conscious life. Their tributaries of thought were all aligned with a central concept that Jung called individuation—the individual's unique purpose unfolding across the lifespan, deeply connected to the collective and bridged to the divine—attenuated through each man's unique form of activism.

Gandhi, King, and Jung each suffered an existential crisis that would catapult them headfirst into a lifetime of suffering and sacrifice for the collective they served. All three were victims of cultural trauma as well—Gandhi and King were persecuted by racism, and Jung suffered the trauma of serving in World War I. Each man faced ridicule and ostracization from various segments of society threatened by what his effort delivered. In his book, *Depth Psychology and the New Ethic*, analytical psychologist Erich Neumann (1990/1969) claimed that great community leaders contribute to the collective through their individual suffering:

Their fate and their often tragic struggle with their problems is of crucial significance for the collective, since both the problem and the solution, the criticism which destroys the old and the synthesis which lays the foundation for the new, are performed by these same individuals for the collective, which, in fact, takes over their work. (pp. 30–31)

Psychoanalyst Erik Erikson was the first psychologist to develop a theory of psychobiology which combines the personal and historical dynamics of a person's life and how these factors affect who they will become. In his book, *Gandhi's Truth: On the Origin of Militant Nonviolence*, Erikson speculated that at the root of Gandhi's nonviolent practice lay an unconscious attempt to manage the guilt he felt regarding his lack of care for his dying father.

In Jungian theoretical terms, Gandhi's nonviolence and dedication to *Satyagraha* and *Ahimsa* expressed a large part of his father complex and laid the foundation for the work that would transform India.

King's father complex defined the nonviolent civil rights leader he would become. The threads of religion, activism, and racism shaped his myth but also intersected with the familial, ancestral, and culturally transgenerational suffering of slavery. King's paternal lineage, father complex and the communal bridge the pulpit created, intertwined to become a force of nature in confronting the country's moral problem of racism.

King's father and grandfather were defined by the racism they regularly experienced and whose retaliation came with a price. In one such case, King's grandfather, Jim King, retaliated against a white millowner who had beaten their young son Michael. When white men on horses showed up at the house for Jim, he fled into the woods where he remained for months (Clayborne Carson, 1992, p. 23). This experience and many more racist encounters shaped Dr. King's life. The pulpit would provide the voice for the transgenerational suffering; nonviolence would become the healing agent and central force within his father complex.

Jung's chosen profession proved to be a combination of his parental complexes. Jung's interest in religion stemmed from his struggle to understand his father's unconditional, but apathetic devotion to his religion; a condition his father refused to address when challenged by the young Carl. Consequently, his father's attitude sparked in Jung a need to understand his apathetic tendencies. Jung's mother Emily, the daughter of a minister as well, was preoccupied with the mystical, spiritual side of life (Bair, 2003, pp. 20–21). Though her father was also a minister, she was not as interested in the dogmatic side of the religion as she was in the underworld. Her interest in the occult stimulated Jung's imagination and desire to understand the soul. His curiosity about his mother would eventually lead to the development of the concept of the *Anima*, the "inner feminine side of a man" (Sharp, 1991, p. 18). The dynamic between the two parental complexes would be the source of Jung's development of his theory of the Self.

Although Gandhi, King and Jung were men of different cultural back-
grounds, linking them is their suffering and the use of their pain as a means to
spiritual transformation. Though they utilized different theoretical languages
in their work, a common thread emerged: the desire to know God, or the Self.

Gandhi and King were born into worlds defined by racism and slavery,
which tore their respective countries into two. Gandhi's India had been over-
run by British rule for hundreds of years, beginning in the 1600s. By 1757,
India had fallen victim to the British East Indian Merchant Company, which
had been given free rein by the British crown to utilize India's natural and
human resources for its benefit. By 1869, India's people had been deeply
physically and psychologically scarred by Britain's colonization. Gandhi
(1962) reported,

> By British figures, approximately four hundred thousand Indians died of
> starvation in the second quarter of the nineteenth century, five million in
> the third quarter, and an appalling fifteen million between 1875 and 1900,
> the years in which Gandhi would come of age. (p. xi)

Born October 2, 1869, Mohandas Karamchand Gandhi was raised in an
upper-caste Indian family which entitled him to the accoutrements of such an
upbringing, including an education and professional career. Gandhi became a
lawyer but could not have known that his professional life would be forever
changed while on a train ride to South Africa when he was systematically
thrown off the train for being Indian. Though Gandhi may have conceptually
understood racism, it was not until that moment that the veil of tolerance was
peeled back, exposing the truth of South African racism towards his kind
and, by association, the whole of his beloved India.

The event in South Africa changed Gandhi profoundly and, seemingly,
overnight. As a result, he vowed to stay in South Africa and fight for the
rights of others. It was through this experimental proclamation that nonviolent philosophy was birthed in Gandhi and delivered into India. In this
fight, "he would not resort to any tactic that would diminish the humanity
he was fighting for. He would cling to the truth and suffer the consequences in trying to 'root out this disease' that was infecting all parties
involved" (Fischer, 1962, p. xix). Gandhi's pursuit of the truth became the
first of a dual prong approach to his nonviolent philosophy, which he
initially coined as the "Civil Resistance" movement (as cited in Fischer,
1951, pp. 88–87).

Gandhi's nonviolent practice enabled him to hold onto the truth, or the
tension of opposites in violent upheavals within himself until a new, third
way emerged. He utilized person and mass demonstrations (e.g., the Salt
March of 1930) or asceticism as a means to uncovering moral truth. Ultimately, Gandhi discovered that peace begins within and that if one cannot
change the darkness within oneself, one cannot contribute to transformation

in the culture. His commitment to freedom for India consolidated a socially and psychologically battered nation into a force of nature consisting of the poorest to the wealthiest India demanding independence from Britain. Gandhi became the carrier of consciousness for his country, which transformed his people and perpetuated a tipping point in India's narrative as a free nation.

Gandhi and King exhibited the capacity to contain inner violence and aggression, thus engendering change in their worlds. According to Gandhi, consciousness equals truth. He professed,

> In the march towards Truth, anger, selfishness and hatred naturally give way, for otherwise Truth would be impossible to attain ... A successful search for Truth means complete deliverance from the dual throng, such as of love and hate, happiness and misery. (1962, p. 4)

Ultimately, Gandhi's constant focus on taming his instinctual urges of power and aggression released him from the affective storms of an ego-driven life and formed the core of his ongoing nonviolent activism. Within the folds of his nonviolent practice emerged the two concepts, *Satyagraha* and *Ahimsa*, which would be the cornerstones to his work, as he believed they contained a divine intelligence. He confessed that at the core of all of his actions was the desire to know God:

> What I want to achieve, –what I have been striving and pining to achieve these thirty years, –is self-realization, to see God face to face to attain *Moksha* [salvation]. I live and move and have my being in pursuit of this goal. All that I do by way of speaking and writing, and all my ventures in the political field, are directed to this same end. (1993, p. xxvi).

Gandhi's nonviolent revolution earned him the name of the "Great Soul," and it eventually won India her independence from Britain via the Indian Independence Act of 1947. One year after the great acclamation, India would lose Gandhi. He was assassinated on January 30, 1948.

Eleven years after Gandhi's death, Martin Luther King, Jr. would conduct a pilgrimage to India in honor of Gandhi and would return to America with a deepened faith in nonviolence, delivering to civil rights a deepened commitment to the practice.

King's name may have been an early indication of what he was to become. His father changed his given Christian name from Michael to Martin Luther at the age of five, setting in motion the archetypal activation of the spiritual revolutionary within King. Born January 16, 1929, Michael King would be ushered into this life by way of the pulpit. The ministry defined his paternal lineage, and despite the many roles he played in society, to the end of his life King would call himself a minister. He stated,

In the quiet recesses of my heart, I am fundamentally a clergyman, a Baptist preacher. This my being and my heritage for I am also the son of a Baptist preacher, the grandson of a Baptist preacher, and the great-grandson of a Baptist preacher. (As cited in Clayborne Carson, 1992, p. 1)

For decades, his family had held the pulpit at Ebenezer Baptist Church, in Atlanta, Georgia, ostensibly defining the world in which young Martin thrived. Christian doctrine and communal integrity provided the image for the core values he would develop, with the intersection between the two shaping his nonviolent ethic. However, the philosophical underpinnings of Christianity and the racism that King encountered proved successful in introducing the young Martin to the cultural sickness from which his family had attempted to protect him. Consequently, King would begin questioning the doctrine and the blind faith to which Christianity ascribed (Clayborne Carson, 1992, pp. 34–35, 361). This questioning would eventually draw him into the theological world, inducing in the adolescent King a generous philosophical thirst for the existential world. He finished high school by the age of 15, where he promptly entered Morehouse College, graduating in 1948 at the age of nineteen. Thereafter, he entered Crozer Theological Seminary in Pennsylvania, where he graduated in 1951 with a baccalaureate degree in divinity. Finally, in 1955, King received his Doctor of Philosophy degree from Boston University. Armed with an exceptional mind and education, King was as prepared as he could be for the challenges he would face.

King grew up in the suburbs of Atlanta, Georgia, in a middle-class, white neighborhood, and made friends with white children with whom he would later be banned from socializing due to his color. King discussed the painful ostracization: "The question arose in my mind, how could I love a race of people who hated me and who had been responsible for breaking me up with one of my best childhood friends?" (as cited in Clayborne Carson, 1992, pp. 31–32). During the civil rights movement, one of King's central messages to protestors would involve the refusal to hate. Holding aggression at bay and refusing to hate had complicated implications for those who did not understand the philosophical roots of the imperative, but for King, this early experience informed his nonviolent practice.

King, like most Southern blacks, encountered racism on a regular basis. His father, a proud and educated man himself, was no exception, but for the fact that he had no qualms about facing down a racist bully. Bearing witness to his father's encounters made an indelible impression upon the young King and would deeply define the man he would become. His father was also an activist, who was an outspoken advocate for the African American's right to vote. Indeed, the church was where much trauma was exposed and processed for blacks. The minister provided the voice for the people as well. King's father utilized the pulpit to heal his community and give voice and vision to his congregants' sufferings. The dream could be heard in King, Sr.'s sermons:

God hasten the time when every minister will become a registered voter and a part of every movement for the betterment of our people. Again, and again has it been said we cannot lead where we do not go, and we cannot teach what we do not know. As ministers a great responsibility rests upon us as leaders. We cannot expect our people to register and become citizens until we, as leaders, set the standard. (As cited in Clayborne Carson, 1992, p. 34)

King, Sr. was a force of nature to young Martin and could also be hard on his son. He was known to whip Martin regularly, emphasizing that he needed his son to understand the forces of racism he was to face in life as a man of color (Garrow, 1986, p. 34). Andrew Young, one of King's lieutenants in the fight for civil rights, stated that it was common in the South for fathers to prepare their young sons for the cruelty of the white world by teaching them to be passive in the face of violence (Kunhardt, 2018, 1:14:22). As part of the complex of racism in the South as well as the trauma, such behaviors enabled young men to survive in the face of white aggression. By the time he marched in Selma, King had long since been groomed in how to react nonviolently in the face of aggression.

By the time he arrived in Montgomery, Alabama, as a 25-year-old, freshly minted minister, King carried with him his education along with a new wife, Coretta, a graduate from Antioch University and an intellectual, musician, and activist who played an instrumental role in Dr. King's success. As the head minister for a robust African American congregation at Dexter Avenue Baptist Church, King barely finished out his first year at the church before his presence extended beyond Montgomery into the nation's living room. Arriving in Montgomery, all seemed relatively calm and predictable despite the burgeoning civil rights revolution swirling around him. King developed a theoretical model for his work behind the pulpit, something which began with his grandfather and became a potent cocktail to social change. King called his ministry a *social-gospel* ministry and believed in "religion as a vehicle for social progress" (Clayborne Carson, 1992, p. 49). King was not interested in the traditional model of Christianity, particularly if it meant that the supplicant practiced only on Sundays. Advocating for religion to effect change in the culture through the transformation of the individual, he stated,

The Christian gospel is a two-way road. On the one hand, it seeks to change the souls of men and thereby unite them with God; on the other hand it seeks to improve the environmental conditions of men so that the soul will have a chance after it is changed. Any religion that professes to be concerned with the souls of men and is not concerned with the slums that damn them, the economic conditions that strangle them, and the social conditions that cripple them is a dry-as-dust religion. (1996/1958, p. 66)

King saw a direct connection between the moral integrity of one's inner and outer worlds. Living a moral life meant following the gospel while working to induce a moral change in one's community through activism and the cultivation of brotherhood. At the core of King's social gospel lay the belief that "God's reality was revealed through the historical unfolding of his moral law" (Clayborne Carson, 1992, p. 49). Racism was one of America's greatest sins; therefore, confronting the moral hypocrisy of racism became the driving force of his nonviolent civil rights campaign. His conviction was so strong that he was willing to be jailed for the sake of collective moral reconciliation. On the television show *Meet the Press*, in 1965, King explained his mandate for nonviolently following moral law for the sake of collective consciousness:

> There at two types of laws. One is a just law, and one is an unjust law. I think we all have the moral obligation to obey just laws. On the other hand, I think we have moral obligation to disobey unjust laws because non-cooperation with evil is as much a moral obligation as is cooperation with the good. I think the distinction here is if one breaks a law that his conscience tells him is unjust, he must do it openly, he must do it cheerfully, he must do it lovingly; he must do it civilly, and he must do it with a willingness to accept the penalty. (King, 1965, 11:20)

Like Gandhi, King believed that holding a consistent nonviolent position in the face of retaliation made conscious the destructive forces ("evil") occluding God's moral law. For King, God was a superordinate power that extended from the personal to the cosmic realm—a creative force that works for universal wholeness. He explained,

> It is true that there are devout believers in nonviolence who find it difficult to believe in a personal God. But even these persons believe in the existence of some creative force that works for universal wholeness. Whether we call it an unconscious process, an impersonal Brahman, or a Personal Being of matchless power and infinite love, there is a creative force in the universe that works to bring disconnected aspects of reality into a harmonious whole. (1958, p. 95)

Like Gandhi before him, King believed that a stand against violence constellates the creative, unifying forces of the universe.

As a doctoral student, King was introduced to Gandhian philosophy through a sermon delivered by Dr. Mordecai Johnson, the President of Howard University. King was so inspired by Gandhi's writings that he immersed himself in nonviolent theory and Gandhi's life story. The development of Gandhi's theory and devotion to nonviolence changed King from a skeptic to a believer. In his autobiography, *Stride Toward Freedom*, King (1958) stated,

> The whole concept of 'Satyagraha' was profoundly significant to me. As I delved deeper into the philosophy of Gandhi, my skepticism concerning the power of love gradually diminished, and I came to see for the first time its potency in the area of social reform. (p. 84).

King's theological studies sharpened his analytical mind, and after studying more than a few philosophers, he homed in on the power of personalism. He wrote,

> I studied personalistic philosophy—the theory that the clue to the meaning of ultimate reality is found in personality. This personal idealism remains today my basic philosophical position. Personalism's insistence that only personality—finite and infinite—is ultimately real, strengthened me in two convictions: it gave me metaphysical and philosophical grounding for the idea of a personal God, and it gave me a metaphysical basis for the dignity and worth of all human personality. (p. 88)

King's personalistic philosophy also ties the strength of the human personality to a unifying energy which joins all of humanity. He asserted, "The Kingdom of God is neither the thesis of individual enterprise nor the antithesis of collective enterprise, but a synthesis which reconciles the truths of both" (p. 83). King iterated Jung's central thesis that human beings are but reflections of a greater unifying force called the archetypal Self. King (1967a) believed that "all life is interrelated. We are all caught in an inescapable network of mutuality, tied into a single garment of destiny" (p.3). Personalism informed King's understanding of the dynamic, transformative potential contained within the individual personality and its effects upon the collective, and he proved this theory effective over and over again in his nonviolent approach to civil rights. What he could not foresee at the time was the opposite effect that his nonviolent movement would have upon the collective and the power of the kickback.

In the last year of King's life, he reflected upon his time during the civil rights movement and admitted that he had been somewhat naive and that the dream he had espoused had turned into a nightmare. Although he felt discouraged, he had not lost his faith, he still believed in the power of nonviolence (King, 1967b, 21:58). Eleven months later, King died. Like Gandhi before him, he was murdered in Memphis, Tennessee on April 5, 1968. Gandhi and King both became the sacrifice for the development of the collective they served.

Carl Gustav Jung was born on July 26, 1875, in the Swiss village of Kesswil. The only son of a Swiss Reformed minister, Jung, like King, grew up in the church. Spirituality and religion played a significant role in young Carl's life. Jung's father, Paul Achilles Jung, was a loving parent who followed the customs of his faith but who did not deeply explore the existential roots of his religion, which puzzled his young son.

Jung's interest in the existential roots of psychological and spiritual life inspired him to enter into the field of psychiatry, then an uncommon choice for medical graduates. However, psychology was a burgeoning science during the early 1900s, with great thinkers such as Sigmund Freud, Pierre Janet, and Jean-Martin Charcot exploring the etiology of the unconscious.

Jung's mother suffered from bouts of depression, which Jung would inherit and experience from an early age (Bair, 2003, pp. 20, 21, 35). His parents had a contentious marriage, which drove Carl to his father's library where he found solace in reading religious and theological texts, perhaps in an unconscious attempt to understand the root causes for his feelings of despair (p. 35). Their bickering aside, the vast differences in his parents' approach to the transpersonal deeply affected Jung and provided the binary religious paradigm from which Jung's depth psychology would form. Perhaps, in the adulthood, the young Carl would reconcile the despair he struggled with as a child. Indeed, his suffering, like King's and Gandhi's, would inspire his work, and ultimately, contribute to the collective psychological development of his culture.

In Jung's early career as a psychiatrist, he worked with schizophrenics, researching the unconscious realm of the psyche. Jung believed that the unconscious was an organ of deep wisdom containing its own unique language (archetypes). As he saw it, the archetypal world, or collective unconscious, connects the individual to the collective through a shared, timeless history that is rooted in the divine mystery of nature, which organized religions called *God* and which Jung defined as the *Self*. He concluded that through exploration via dreams, fantasies, and myths, human beings can develop a relationship with the inner self, which can be experienced through an inner pilgrimage known as the *individuation process*. Jung believed that the individuation process could be contained best in the practice of analysis, whereby the individual utilizes the analytic process as a telos in which the full personality can organically unfold. Jung's idea of consciousness is a form of inner activism extending into the intrapsychic world, whereby attaining transformation of inner violence is the only way of effecting the transformation of violence in the outer world.

Jung questioned whether a human being's destiny is predetermined or imprinted, or if a human comes into the world as a *tabula rasa*, a blank slate. Ultimately, he determined that humans are influenced by the ages or the archetypal world, bringing into the world a set of psychic patterns, or archetypes, embedded and ready for activation. Which archetypes become constellated depends on the personal and cultural conditions into which one is born and exposed throughout one's lifespan (1998, pp. 158–159).

The process of individuation can be seen as an instinctually driven form of adaptive activism within and between one's ego, self, and culture. One discovers one's identity as one's ego is continuously deconstructed and reconstituted in the face of personal and cultural limitations and potentialities all guided by the center of the personality, the Self. This process is the painful but central experience of shadow integration. Following shadow integration is the seminal phase of one's surrendering to something greater, the (s)Self. The individual self can be seen as an offshoot of the higher Self embedded in the individual personality, and which develops along with the ego, until the higher Self appears. With the Self as the central motif in the Jungian lexicon, Jung's writings on evil seemingly circumambulated his wonderings about the Self, enforcing its existence and purpose in the human experience. Jung (1960) expounded on the locus of evil in his book, *Answer to Job: The Problem of Evil: Its Psychological and Religious Origins*. Ultimately, Jung contended that good and evil are aspects in all of nature, including God's, and that the dark side is as real as the light side. Jung wondered about the interdependent relationship between God and human beings. He speculated that God could be made more conscious in humans or develop through an individual's attainment of a conscious life. The archetypal expression of the God-image is thus directly related to the individual's capacity to understand and recognize shadow and, through its integration, pave the way for a relationship with the Self.

Unlike Jung, Gandhi did not believe that God contained darkness; only humans were evil. As reflected in the following statement, he believed in the benevolence of God:

> For I can see in the midst of death that life persists, in the midst of untruth, truth persists, in the midst of darkness light persists. Hence, I gather that God is Life, Truth, Light. He is Love. He is Supreme Good. (Prahu and Rao, 1998, p. 77)

Gandhi believed it to be humans' exclusive responsibility to root out evil, because they are the root of evil. Gandhi's nonviolent aestheticism and practice was designed to purge or cleanse himself of his violent tendencies in order to know God.

Like Gandhi and King, Jung struggled with the question of evil. Just as violence and nonviolence are intertwined, so are evil and goodness. One can begin discerning good from evil by questioning the validity of what is considered a projection, the source material for potential evil and goodness. A projection is the expelling of an inner subjective experience onto an outer condition or person. The development of consciousness includes one's recognition of this projection, and the subsequent retraction of the projection thereby induces appropriate feelings of shame or humiliation for the faulty belief or behavior that lives within. The process of self-reflection, ironically, often requires the lens of the other to reveal or reflect the nature of one's shadow. According to Jung, the spread of evil,

> begins with the lie, the projection of the shadow ... There is need of people knowing about their shadow, because there must be somebody who does not project. They ought to be in a visible position where they would be expected to project and unexpectedly they do not project! They can thus set a visible example which would not be seen if they were invisible. (As cited in Stein, 1995, p. 77)

Nonviolent philosophy addresses that which contributes to evil, thus confronting the ego's faulty psychological constructs through a refusal of violence. Consequently, as discussed shortly regarding the civil rights protest in Selma, the individual's choice of facing down evil can ultimately affect collective health as well. King's understanding of evil is similar to Jung's: The one affects the many, and activism, in the form of nonviolent consciousness, is essential in truncating the spread of evil. King (1958) declared,

> He who passively accepts evil is as much involved in it as he who helps to perpetrate it. He who accepts evil without protesting against it is cooperating with it. When oppressed people willingly accept their oppression, they only serve to give the oppressor a convenient justification for his acts. Often the oppressor goes along, unaware of the evil involved in his oppression so long as the oppressed accepts it. So in order to be true to one's conscience and true to God, a righteous man has no alternative but to refuse to cooperate with an evil system. (p. 39)

Jung also believed that the collective shadow is constellated through denial, irresponsibility, and neglect of self through ego-centricity and hubris. Jungian analyst Murray Stein (1998), in his book, *Encountering Jung: Jung on Evil*, discussed the direct connection between the individual and culture and the development of consciousness as a remedy for collective disease. He wrote,

> For human cultures to transform, each individual must grapple with the inner forces of good and evil and must confront the demon of ego-centricity, whether this is defined by one's own immediate physical existence or by the tribal group or national interests. (p. 67)

Cultural transformation can be truly effective only when those within the zeitgeist are transforming their individual psyches; otherwise, the process only contributes to the formation of a false self, which can easily crumble when tested.

For Gandhi, King, and Jung, the transpersonal realm of existence is the place where God or Self resides; it is the fulcrum to healing for the ego. In *The*

Red Book, Jung's seminal, personal treatise on the psyche's alchemical processes, he stated, "Two things remain to be discovered. The first is the infinite gulf that separates us from one another. The second is the bridge that could connect us" (2009, p. 289). With over sixty years of professional life dedicated to the field of psychology, Carl Jung died at his home in Küsnacht, Switzerland, on June 6, 1961.

References

Bair, D. (2003). *Jung A Biography*. Boston, New York, London: Little, Brown and Company.

Clayborne Carson, E. (2005). *The Papers of Martin Luther King, Jr. Volume V, Threshold of a New Decade January 1959-December 1960*. Berkley, Los Angeles, London: University of California Press.

Clayborne Carson, S. E. (1992). *The Papers of Martin Luther King, Jr. Volume 1, Called To Serve January 1929-June 1951*. Stanford: University of California Press.

Erikson, E. (1969). *Gandhi's Truth: on the Origin of Militant Nonviolence*. New York: Norton & Company.

Fischer, L. (1951). *The Life of Mahatma Gandhi*. New York: Harper & Brothers.

Fischer, L. (ed.) (1962). *The Essential Gandhi: an Anthology of His Writings on His Life, Work and Ideas*. New York, Toronto: Random House Publications.

Gandhi, M. (1962). *The Essential Gandhi: An Anthology of His Writings on His Life, Work, and Ideas*. New York: Vintage Spiritual Classics.

Gandhi, M. K. (1993). *An Autobiography: The Story of My Experiments with Truth*. Boston: Beacon Press.

Garrow, D. (1986). *Bearing the Cross*. New York: Perennial Classics.

Jung, C. G. (1939). *The Integration of the Personality*. New York, Toronto: Farrar and Rinehart.

Jung, C. G. (1960). *Answer to Job The Problem of Evil: Its Psychological and Religious Origins*, translated by R. F. C. Hull. Cleveland, New York: Meridian Books, The World Publishing Company.

Jung, C. (2009). *The Red Book, A Reader's Edition*. New York: Norton.

King Jr., Martin Luther (1958). *Stride Toward Freedom: the Montgomery Story*. Boston: Beacon Press.

King, M. L. (1965, March 28). Meet The Press. (L. E. John Chancellor, Interviewer) *National Broadcasting Company. NBC*, New York. Retrieved from https://www.youtube.com/watch?v=fAtsAwGreyE.

King, M. L. (1967a, December 24). http://www.thekingcenter.org/archive/document/christmas-sermon#. Retrieved from thekingcenter.org: http://www.thekingcenter.org.

King, M. L. (1967b). *National Broadcasting Company* (Sander Vanocur, Interviewer). Retrieved from https://youtu.be/2xsbt3a7K-8.

King, M. L. (1996/1958). *The Words of Martin Luther King, Jr.* 2nd edition, C. S. King (ed.). New York: New Market Press.

Kunhardt, P. (Director). (2018). *King in the Wilderness* [Motion Picture].

Neumann, E. (1990/1969). *Depth Psychology and the New Ethic*. Boston: Shambala Publications.

Petri, Fabrizio (2014). Gandhi, Jung and Nonviolence Today The Relevance of the Feminine in the Network Society. *II Quarterly*, 41(1), 7–18.

Prahu, R. K. and Rao, U. R. (1998). *The Mind of Mahatma Gandhi Encyclopedia of Gandhi's Thoughts.* Ahmedabad, India: Jitendra T. Desai.

Sharp, Daryl (1991). *C.G. Jung Lexicon A Primer of Terms & Concepts.* Toronto: Inner City Books.

Stein, M. (1995). *Encountering Jung: Jung on Evil, 1995 Selected and Introduced by Murray Stein.* Princeton: Princeton University Press.

Stein, Murray (1998). *Jung's Map of the Soul an Introduction.* Chicago: Open Court Press.

Storr, A. (1983). *The Essential Jung.* Princeton: Princeton University Press.

Chapter 4

Archetypal nonviolence

Two dogs dance together within their pen house, each moving in harmony with the other. Dodging and darting around the other's body, each dog simultaneously smells and licks the other, negotiating a complicated contract of dominance and submission. To the human eye the dogs appear as if they are playing, yet something more instinctual and complex is happening. As one dog quickens its pace leaning into the other just so slightly, the more aggressive dog's tail becomes extended high into the air, a bid for dominance. The more dominant dog seems to be on the edge of an aggressive attack, the air crackling with a desire-laced aggression morphing from one moment to the next into a language known only between them, unpredictable and yet, charged. Just in the nick of time, a third dog, the alpha, enters the pack. This interlocutor steps in to titrate the more aggressive dog's moves, as if to say, "check yourself." Cutting in between the other two dogs the alpha tethers himself to the more dominant canine becoming its shadow, his body mediating the aggressive energies being exchanged between the other two canines.

The alpha presses his body in on the more dominant dog, signaling his authority. Indeed, the alpha is performing a nonviolent maneuver of adaptation being negotiated within the pack. In a few moments, the more aggressive dog settles down, clearly receiving the message from the alpha, a new understanding emerging between the three dogs. In response, the third dog surrenders to his more gregarious counterpart by lying down. A physical altercation avoided, a bid for dominance resolving itself into a hierarchical understanding agreed upon by all participants. And while this is not always the case, the capacity for peaceful negotiations among the group has been demonstrated effectively (Considerthedog.com).

For animals nonviolence is a process utilized to encourage adaptation within the pack, establishing a hierarchy whereby all can survive peacefully, together, their social coding embedded deeply within their behavioral DNA. For canines, the role of the dominant and submissive is negotiated in play and constantly changes based on who most desires the dominant role. In humans, the process of adaptation works in a similar fashion.

While civil rights demonstrations periodically erupted into violence, for the most part, King, like the alpha dog in the pack, attempted to contain and non-violently persuade his persecutors to turn away from violence, to check them-selves, to engage in the use of nonviolence as a means of adapting or integrating the races. Like Gandhi before him, King's nonviolence demanded equal rights for all races and was utilized as a spiritual weapon to break through petrified hierarchical barriers used to oppress African Americans for centuries. In *Stride Toward Freedom*, he states the goal of nonviolence was "not to defeat the white man, but to awaken a sense of shame within the oppressor and challenge his false sense of superiority" (1958, p. 81). He believed oppression of the races could be confronted through nonviolent activism, and a new moral order restored through the refusal of hate and violence. Nonviolence as a spiritual practice provides a nonsectarian, non-religious ethos which can be utilized to cultivate, restore and maintain peace through the development of consciousness.

Nonviolence is a state of mind and heart that directly addresses violence by using thought, word, and deed in such a way as to dissolve, break apart, and transmute violence from chaos to ordered energy. Mark Kurlansky, in his book *Nonviolence: The History of a Dangerous Idea* (2006), states that "while every major language has a word for violence, there is no word to express the idea of nonviolence" (p. 5).

Gandhi (1962) states that the closest terminology to nonviolence comes from the Sanskrit word *Ahimsa*. "*Ahimsa* is a derivative of the word *himsa,* which means to harm ... Important to Hinduism and Buddhism, *Ahimsa* is the com-plete absence of violence in word and even thought as well as action" (p. xxv). *Ahimsa* is a philosophical, spiritual stance that is evolutionary in nature and can never truly be achieved (Kurlansky, 2006; Gandhi, 1962). "Nonviolence is a perfect stage. It is a goal towards which all humanity moves naturally, though unconsciously" (Gandhi, 1962, p. xxv). "In Taoism *teh* is a perfection of nature, and, as in Hinduism, is something few people have the strength and character to live up to" (p. 12). Yet, there is in Taoism the notion that more conscious beings are less violent, making the practice of nonviolence a compelling anti-dote to instinctual violent urgings. Gandhi affirmed this notion and encouraged the practice of nonviolence as a tamer of one's inner aggression. In *The Essen-tial Gandhi: An Anthology of His writings on Life, Work, and Ideas* (1962), he states: "I have learnt through bitter experience the one supreme lesson to con-serve my anger, and as heat conserved is transmuted into energy, even so our anger controlled can be transmuted into a power which can move the world" (p. xxii). Infuse a violent experience with nonviolent con-sciousness, and you have a recipe for peace.

In the Chinese language, the word closest to nonviolence is *teh*. "In Taoism, there is a concept embodied in the *teh*. Not exactly nonviolence, which is an active force, *teh* is the virtue of not fighting—nonviolence is the path to *teh.*" (Kurlansky, 2006, p. 11). Ultimately, *teh*, like *Ahimsa*, is a state that cannot be perfected but can be pursued through a path of nonviolence.

Gandhi referred to consciousness as *Satyagraha*. "*Satyagraha*—literally 'holding on to Truth'—is the name he coined for his method of fighting without violence or retaliation." (Gandhi, 1962, p. xxiv). The application of *Satyagraha* supports consciousness and counteracts the influence(s) of evil.

> It means, that evil is real only insofar as we support it. The essence of holding on to truth is to withdraw support of what is wrong. If enough people do this from a great enough depth—evil has to collapse from lack of support. (p. xxiv)

Satyagraha provides the *active* activism in nonviolent philosophy, where *ahimsa* supports the study and practice of nonviolent harm to self and other. "*Ahimsa* is unconditional love; *satyagrahaa* is love in action."

While Gandhi did not support violence, he detested pacifism even more, for he viewed it as a potential impetus to violence. "There is hope for a violent man to become nonviolent. There is no such hope for the impotent" (Kurlansky, 2006, p. 149). *Satyagraha*, or truth force, could meet violence through the assertion of will. In its practice nonviolence is as forceful as violence and contains the potential to shift the spiritual landscape within an individual or culture.

According to Kurlansky, the one word that comes close to fitting *satyagraha* and *ahimsa* is the Islamic term *jihad*, which means "nonviolent activism." In the Quran, the term *jihad* "originally meant to strive with great intensity for a relationship with Allah. However, this striving was supposed to be an internal struggle to become the perfect Muslim that God-Allah-wanted each Muslim to be" (p. 36). Unfortunately, in the term *jihad*, the paradigm of the internal struggle is misunderstood as an outer goal of converting the other to Islam, in the name of Allah/God. In its essence, however, the word *jihad* supports the journey of nonviolent activism, an inner ethic which mirrors the process of psychological individuation (p. 36).

Gandhi's life revolved around the sacred mystery of the soul's transcendent potential. His life's dedication was to the forces of the divine mystery of the relationship between God and man. While seemingly erudite and unattainable, Gandhi was confident that the goal of this mystery was founded in being fully human through the spiritual pursuit of a nonviolent life. According to Mairead Corrigan Maguire, in *Peace is the Way* (Wink, 2000),

> Gandhi realized that the spirit of nonviolence begins within us and moves out from there. The life of nonviolence is the fruit of an inner peace and spiritual unity already realized in us and not the other way around ... Herein lies the power of nonviolence. As our hearts are disarmed by God of our inner violence, they become God's instruments for the disarmament of the world (p. 159).

Down to the finest detail, Gandhi pursued nonviolence physically, emotionally and psychologically, devoting himself exclusively to the pursuit of God through truth and love. He consumed no foods obtained through violent means, he dressed in the barest of physical essentials, clothing himself with his own spun cloth. Gandhi built a temenos defined of spiritual, physical and mental contemplation, defined by humility and sacrifice vigilantly attempting to bring his world into communion with God:

> There is an indefinable mysterious Power that pervades everything. I feel it, though I do not see it. It is this unseen Power that makes itself felt, and yet defies all proof, because it is unlike all that I perceive through my senses. It transcends the senses. I do dimly perceive that whilst everything around me is ever changing, ever dying there is underlying all that change a Living Power that is changeless, that holds all together, that creates dissolves and recreates. That informing spirit or Power is God. (Ajgaonkar, 1995, p. 60)

God as a cosmic force, or "living Power that is changeless that holds all together," coincides with Jung's concept of the archetypal Self. The self's relationship within the individual is a dynamic process which unfolds throughout the lifespan. It is through the process of becoming that the personality is cyclically created, dissolved, coagulated and re-constituted through the waters of violence and nonviolence. The same process occurs in culture whereby the individual and culture form a fulcrum of development from which the archetypal Self also emerges. The self is an archetype of wholeness which contains transpersonal properties and serves as a binding agent or ordering factor for all of the personality. The ego is constantly being shaped by the self through experiences defined by engulfment to assimilation. The Self also constitutes all archetypes. Therefore, the self is not just the center of the individual personality, from which all experiences extend and are ordered, but constitutes the entire archetypal world containing all conscious and unconscious experiences and beyond.

How life itself manifests into a culture can be seen in the calibrating process between violence and nonviolence. Does life emerge from the movement of violence to nonviolence, or are these forces inextricably bound together, such that the ordering mechanism is a consciousness that can be both violent and nonviolent? Perhaps it is all of the above. Violence and nonviolence are instinctive and archetypal life force energies that are intricately and inextricably intertwined, and whose coupling form the syzygy, or union of opposites. The intrapsychic struggle between violence and nonviolence is fundamental to human nature and forms the dynamism from which the mythopoeic narrative of life emerges. Archetypal nonviolence mediates the urge to annihilate creating space for a psychic third to emerge, a subjective experience informed by the transcendent function. Within the third one can choose relatedness in its variant forms, over the urge to objectify the other by psychologically, emotionally or bodily dominating, or destroying the object.

According to Fabrizio Petri, in his article "Gandhi, Jung and Nonviolence Today" (2014), *Ahimsa*, the practice of nonviolent love is an interpersonal commitment to transform the inner and outer worlds; "to innovate entirely without revolution; and to deeply transform the present without disregarding the past" (p. 8). Nonviolence submits a new ethic that offers all participants of the violent paradigm something other than oppression, dominance and humiliation, for nonviolence deeply affects all parties involved. It addresses the fundamental rupture in the paradigm of relationship; either intrapsychically between the ego and the self, or in the outer world, with another.

In animals, this may be witnessed as an adaptation problem resulting in pack violence. For humans, it is a disruption in our capacity to see and experience the other as fully human. Objectification of the other cultivates disequilibrium, setting in motion a power paradigm increasing the likelihood for conflict and violence. The implementation of nonviolence can procure a peace infused *agape*, or divine love, one of our deepest instinctual experiences. Through nonviolent intervention one's refusal of violence and aggression sheds light on the urge to power within the other. Through the study of a nonviolent ethos we can learn a lot about why humans choose war as a means of expression and desire peace and love as well. Perhaps humans choose war as a means of expression because they have not achieved the ability to bind affect into symbol, thus short-circuiting the capacity to effectively communicate aggression. Archetypal nonviolence can provide the codifying mechanism necessary for the emergence of a language formed through consciousness. Jungian scholar Andrew Samuels, in his book *Jung and the Post-Jungians* (1985), discussed the Self as a mediating force of nature that works as an open system delivering to the human realm something equal to and greater than the first primary experience of love; such as in the mother–infant relationship. Further, he surmises that the self,

> *can* be viewed in terms of relationship with others. The self is the primary source of phenomena such as empathy. Human capacity to put oneself in the shoes of another implies something more than an extrapolation from self-referent data, which is then applied to the situation of others. Empathy is a form of psychological interpenetration, a deep link between people; the mother-infant relationship is both a special example of this and a model for empathy throughout life. We are talking of ways in which people absorb the lessons of experience and this, it may be argued, depends on the sense-making capacity of the self which is more than ego-learning (p. 99).

Archetypal nonviolence as the relational bridge creates the environment and the means for empathy when violence threatens psychic integration of the self, and as such, bridges the personal to the transpersonal Self. Samuels enforces this notion: "A further function in connection with self and others concerns the tendency to seek a merger with something 'greater' than oneself." Nonviolence forms such a bridge (p. 99).

Jungian analyst James Hillman discusses the human being's proclivity for violence and war in his book *A Terrible Love of War* (2004). In examining mythology and the archetypal patterns embedded in myth, Hillman brings attention to the relationship of love and war as they are expressed in the coupling of Mars and Venus, a relationship in which love and war cannot be parsed because they are intertwined. "Mars and Venus are always in the bed of the image, even when the tale says they fly off and away from each other. They remain an inseparable conjunction" (p. 109). They are the primary forces of nature. Nonviolent activism brings into focus our "terrible love of war" as well as providing options to violence through reason, nonviolent action and the demand for peace.

As Hillman surmises, the result of the very painful union of love and war gives birth to Harmonia, the mythical child birthed from the union of Ares (God of War) and Venus (Goddess of love). The marriage of these forces in their variant forms provides the algorithm(s) to the deepest mysteries of life. One could ask then how the tenets of nonviolence serve nature in her deepest most divine expression, because while humans are aggressive and violent, we are also exceedingly altruistic. Indeed, there is current research which suggests that we are living in the most peaceful time in human history (WGBH, 2019). And that while we have the resources to self-destruction through war, there exists a compensatory relationship between the *means* of violence and the necessity of avoiding violence.

Wars encourage regression; psychological splitting, projection and tribalism. Yet, our greatest war globally sits at the crest of the battlefield informed by centuries of nature's neglect. It is a war for which humans are unprepared—it is eco-cide. This kind of war requires a dismantling of tribalism and calls for a greater collective union, coupled with political spiritual warfare designed to bring global awakening through an eco-soul consciousness. Thus, spiritual or philosophical nonviolence is mankind's urgent call back to the source, the soul, for the development of a consciousness of a different kind. It is a call to the collective ego's return to the Self. Such a warfare has been primed by three great teachers, Gandhi, King and Jung.

Gandhi's concepts of *Satyagraha* and *Ahimsa* provide the crucible for the containment of violence, and work together as foundational principles for Martin Luther King, Jr's. six nonviolent tenets. In his book *Stride Towards Freedom* (1958), King lists his six tenets: "nonviolence is not a passive non-resistance to evil, but an active resistance to evil" (p. 90); "nonviolence does not seek to humiliate the opponent, but to win his friendship and understanding" (p. 91); "nonviolence is directed at the forces of evil rather than against persons who happen to be doing evil" (p. 91); "the nonviolent resister is willing to accept violence if necessary, but never to inflict it" (p.92); "non-violence avoids not only external violence but also internal violence of spirit" (p. 92); "nonviolence is based on the conviction that the universe is on the side of justice" (p. 95). Together, Gandhi and King's nonviolent tenets form the eightfold path of nonviolence.

During the civil rights movement nonviolence defined two schools of thought existing on a continuum. On one end was tactical nonviolence uti-lized to confront oppression and resolve racism. Examples of tactical non-violence included singing, silence, publicity, marching arm-to-arm, physically surrendering to violence, as well as jailing (Hartford, 2004/1963, p. 1). In the Selma marches of 1965, the implementation of these tactics constellated the hidden aggressions of the town's sheriff, James (Jim) Clark, bringing out into the open his racist views. Indeed, nonviolence does not create aggression, it only reveals the unconscious patterns which consciously propagate the experience. Tactics encourage the revelation. Demonstrators who imple-mented strategic nonviolence were trained to withstand the retaliatory attacks

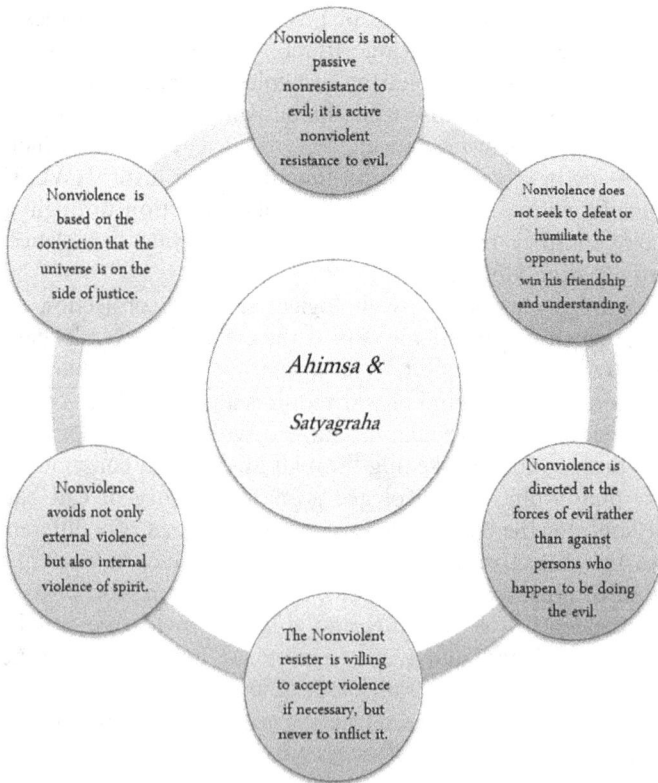

Figure 4.1 The Eightfold Path of Nonviolence: Mahatma Gandhi's Two Foundational Principles and Martin Luther King, Jr.'s Six Tenets

of racists without responding violently. While many did not agree with, or could not attain King's philosophical stance (Hartford, 2004/1963, p. 1), they participated in the struggle because they believed they could tip over the violent social structures of racism through nonviolent strategy. To seduce the oppressor into engaging in an enactment of violence is called tactical coercion.

Bruce Hartford, a nonviolent activist in the 1960s, wrote about the difficulty of holding both the philosophical and tactical nonviolent positions: "Those of us who were tactically nonviolent did not love our enemies, nor did we believe that our redemptive suffering would convert racists and segregationists to a new outlook on interracial brotherly love. Rather than changing hearts, our focus was changing behavior through persuasion, if possible, but if that was not possible then by coercion" (Hartford, 2004/1963, p. 1). Tactical nonviolence politically affected change. The shadow side of tactical nonviolence is an urge to power to gain control over an opponent for the purposes of winning a political position. Without consciousness, tactical nonviolence may contribute to more violence and aggression, because both the nonviolent activist and opponent can easily get caught in a power paradigm unconsciously setting in motion violent archetypal defenses within the complex, thus, fortifying the split. According to Hartford:

> Those who were tactically nonviolent used Nonviolent Resistance as a tool for building political power — in demonstrations, as an organizing technique & style, and as a political strategy to achieve specific goals. But it was a tactic, not a philosophy of life; and in other situations — both personal and political — other strategies and tactics might be used. We who were tactically nonviolent used Nonviolent Resistance because we wanted to win. (Hartford, 2004/1963, p. 1)

Tactical nonviolent participants formed the backbone of the demonstrations working on the front lines to manifest a new dream carried by all but implemented philosophically through the movement's leaders. The spectrum of nonviolent activism moved from the need to win by any nonviolent means necessary, to the philosophical end of the spectrum that encompassed the need to be in agapeic communion with human nature via a nonviolent relationship with the other.

King and his lieutenants formed the spiritual core of the movement and contained the capacity to deliver abstinence from violence in the face of tremendous provocation from opponents. They provided emotional, psychological and spiritual support, both through participating in the demonstrations themselves, while also transcribing the philosophy via the pulpit through prayer and practice.

The philosophical leaders of the movement believed in the ability of God's love (*Agape*) and its transformative powers. They subscribed to *Agape* and the notion that the creation of culture was at hand through the work of God. According to King (1958), "The Holy Spirit is the continuing community creating reality that moves through history. He who works against the community is working against the whole of creation" (p. 94).

Jungian psychology's archetypal Self is similar to Christianity's idea of God. Yet, the Self is also vastly different, for it is cosmic. The Self is the binding agent within nature which orchestrates the endless symphonies contained therein and which is nature herself. The understanding and implementation of this idea through nonviolent philosophy meant that the nonviolent practitioner be able to value the soul and spirit of the other by rebuking physical and spiritual violence. Thus, nonviolence contributes to the communal creation of *Agape*.

According to Hartford, the philosophical approach was difficult, and those who could hold both strategic and philosophical positions were few:

> Those who were philosophically nonviolent did try to love their enemies and did try to refrain from any form of violence in all aspects of their lives. Politically they were pacifists and deeply studied in Gandhian creed. Dr. King, John Lewis, James Lawson, Bernard LaFayette, and others belonged to this group. The heart of philosophical nonviolence was taking action to oppose injustice and winning over one's enemies through love and redemptive suffering. Yet, despite the media myths, philosophical nonviolents were always a small minority of the Civil Rights Movement. (Hartford, 2004/1963, p. 1)

Gandhi and King, among a few others, could hold the philosophical stance, for this required an extraordinary capacity for suffering and a deeply held faith in the powers of spiritual transformation. Theirs was a practice aimed towards healing the collective, whereas the strategists were concerned solely with winning over their oppressors. According to Hartford, both ends of the spectrum held when brought together, even though the demonstrators may have had different capacities to hold violence. Again, Hartford:

> These two views were not hostile to each other — they were just different. Both groups worked well together, simply agreeing to respectfully disagree. Dr. King made it quite clear that he was not demanding that others adopt his personal philosophy of nonviolence, and we who were tactically nonviolent respected the courage and commitment of the philosophicals. The two views were not antagonistic because both encompassed the fundamental premise that nonviolence is about active resistance — not passivity. (p. 1)

The civil rights leaders who had the unique capacity to hold the tension of nonviolent truth in the face of violence were able to shift racism from the physical realm, where the problem affected only a few, to the spiritual realm where the nation at large was forced to face its gravest moral problem.

Nonviolent protestors on both ends of the spectrum formed a line of defense against violence and unitarily functioned together as peace activists, working skillfully to win over their opponents, ultimately transforming violence. Each nonviolent act was unique, based on a confluence of factors because each act confronted violence accordingly. Hartford states: "Nonviolent direct action is like fine jazz. Flair of improvisational creativity, never the same twice, your sound, my sound, our harmony. But harmony requires unity & discipline. The ensemble, not the soloist" (Hartford, 2004/ 1963, p. 1). Through the group of protestors nonviolence uniquely offers itself up to violence, challenging the inflictors to question their motives, effectiveness and purpose.

King's six nonviolent tenets form the philosophical base matter of the theory. Each tenet challenges its practitioner to contemplate their human capacity to love and forgive. There is a sacred mystery in what comes from one's ability to work through both the tendency toward violence and one's deepest need for love. King's six tenets challenge us to hold steadfast to the desire for a relationship in the face of one's domination or urge to power. For those whom it is an abiding philosophy, nonviolence is the endless pursuit of inner peace, it is a demand for love.

King's first tenet defines nonviolence as an active psychological and emotional process: Nonviolence is "not a passive nonresistance to evil, but an active nonviolent resistance to evil" (King, 1958, p. 90). In 1965 the Selma protestors had to be tactically consistent, forceful and persistently creative in coercing their opponent into surrendering their oppressive behavior(s). Nonviolent activism peels back the layers of the complex exposing shadow. Kozu Haga quotes King:

> We who engage in nonviolent direct action are not the creators of the tension. We merely bring to the surface the hidden tension that is already alive. WE bring it out in the open, where it can be seen and dealt with. Like a boil that can never be cured so long as it is covered up but must be opened with its ugliness to the natural medicines of air and light. Injustice must be exposed, with all the tension its exposure creates, to the light of human conscience and the air of national opinion before it be cured. (Haga, 2015)

In King's second tenet he emphasized the democratic process of building relationships designed to reveal a truth devoid of humiliation but built through mutual human kinship. His second tenet states: "Nonviolence does not seek to humiliate the opponent, but to win his friendship and understanding" (King, 1958, p. 91). According to Bernard Lafayette, a lieutenant in King's Southern Christian Leadership Conference, nonviolence was indeed a radical idea, for while the goal of nonviolence was to cultivate peace through the alchemy of truth, the method could be strident in its persistent pursuit to flip the opponent. According to Lafayette:

> The nonviolent approach is radical enough to (for one to) believe that under the worse conditions there is hope. It is radical enough (for one) to believe that people who display the most insensitive kind of attitudes can be changed. The ultimate goal is to win your opponents over. So that you had to psychologically disarm them. You had to confront your opponent and look your opponent in the eye so that they would not see you as the target but as the human being you are … forcing your humanity on them. (Kunhardt, 2018, 37:00)

King always demonstrated the unique capacity to win over his opponents through his abiding understanding of people and his capacity to communicate to even the most depraved hearts. He understood the bully mentality, a core trait of the extraverted racist. King knew that at some point in a bully's life, they must bury the dream of belonging to a loving family. King's radical philosophy of love through militant nonviolence provided the spiritual weapon to not only out the bully but to return him to the fold of the human community.

Andrew Young, also a close companion of King, recalled a particularly contentious trip to Illinois where the Southern Christian Leadership Conference (SCLC) were protesting for the rights of the poor; specifically, for low-income housing in the city of Chicago. The tension in the environment was sprung tightly around racial and social injustice, not just for blacks but for the poor in general. Unprepared for the level of racist vitriol in the streets of Chicago, King and his colleagues closed ranks but persistently marched in keeping with their goals. Surrounded and practically chased through the streets by angry mobs of white racists, King barely flinched in the face of the physical threats to his life.

At some point during the protests, Andrew Young recalled King being ridiculed and spat on by an angry white woman. Despite the humiliating and rage-filled moment, King stopped, looked her in the eyes and said; "You know, you're much too beautiful to be so mean" (Kunhardt, 2018, 36:30). Later that same day, as the group circled back in her direction, the vengeful white woman approached King again, this time apologizing; "I never should have been so rude" (Kunhardt, 2018, 37:00). In the face of such hatred, King's compassion and patience could win over his opponents. He understood that to win the opponent's understanding required persistence through continued good will. He never gave up on his belief that peace lived on the other side of conflict and is obtained through persistence and patience. He asserted that the continued good will of the nonviolent demonstrator contributed to cultivating reconciliation between and within the oppressed and the oppressor. King would later admit to his friend Harry Belafonte that racism in the

North was more challenging and more hate-filled than in the South, because it was subverted (Kunhardt, 2018, 16:00), thus challenging the activists capacity to contain the racial vitriol that their nonviolence uncovered.

One of King's greatest characteristics was his ability to look beyond the persona, or mask of the individual, straight into their soul. He believed that through nonviolent warfare the individual and culture could be redeemed from the effects of what King called the three great American evils: racism, militarism, and poverty (Kunhardt, 2018, 7:15).

Nonviolent warfare is a spiritual practice which challenges the practitioner's instinctual urges to dominate and control, inviting into consciousness another way of behaving and relating through nonviolence. King's third tenet states that "nonviolence is directed at the forces of evil rather than against persons who happen to be doing the evil" (King, 1958, p. 91). The nonviolent way induces reflection both within the practitioner and hopefully, within the recipient, aimed at reducing evil without condemning the other as such. Ostensibly, this principle respects the individual while condemning their destructive behavior.

King's definition of evil was rooted in Christian theology. Evil, therefore, was generally seen as behavior conducted on a spectrum from unconscious to conscious depravity, void of goodness. Yet, King believed in the soul's redemption, even in the face of evil. For the purposes of this book, evil will be used similarly to the Jungian notion of shadow, where goodness exists within the folds of shadow, and not pure depravity without consciousness.

As nonviolent leaders both King and Gandhi believed that the opponent must always be treated with dignity and respect with the condemnation of their behavior being the focus of attention because if the opponent feels demeaned their ego can retaliate in violence (Kurlansky, 2006, p. 146). For violence to end, the opponent must be made to see that their violent behavior is maladaptive instead. This is a tricky proposal at best and must be implemented with the surety of a samurai.

Many African American benefactors of the racist South could not understand the kindness and compassion of King. His refusal to hate in the face of violence was astounding to them. Malcolm X and Stokely Carmichael were a few of the African American leaders who emerged during the civil rights movement that demanded revenge. And while he would eventually march with Stokely Carmichael, King did not agree with Carmichael's violent philosophy. For King, mutual violence only led to annihilation. For King, someone had to wage a different kind of war, a war which harnessed aggression and rage transforming it productively.

Psychiatrist Nassir Ghaemi in his book *First Rate Madness*, discussed the demonstrator's implementation of nonviolence and the use of aggression as a tool for psychological transformation. He cited Harry Belafonte's knowledge of Kingian nonviolence: "Martin always felt that anger was a very important commodity, a necessary part of the black movement in this country" (2011, p. 112). Furthermore Ghaemi states,

> Nonviolence is not about being nonaggressive; it is about being aggressive in a nonviolent way. Rage is natural, part of being human; one cannot deny it without painful psychic consequences. But rage can be channeled in a constructive manner, going outside insofar as it resists injustice, and going inward insofar as it supports the higher courage needed to suffer rather than inflict suffering. This cure for racism benefits both the oppressed and the oppressor. (p. 112).

King's capacity to understand the transformative properties of aggression was no more evident than in his relationship with Laurie Pritchett, the police chief of Albany, Georgia. After the success of the Montgomery bus boycotts in 1956, King brought his demonstrations to Albany to protest. The protests were consistent, powerful and exhausting for all involved, including Pritchett. The demonstrators were so persistent that at one point, Pritchett had to move into a downtown apartment in order to effectively deal with the marches. One afternoon, King, noticing that Pritchett looked particularly exhausted, inquired as to Pritchett's health. Pritchett admitted to King that he was tired, and moreover was in trouble at home for his extended absences. On the day in question, Pritchett was particularly worried about not being home because it was his wedding anniversary. King's compassion and understanding for Pritchett as well as their mutual struggles in being away from their families contributed to King's next move. King struck a bargain with Pritchett; if he would go home and celebrate his marriage with his wife, King would hold off on protesting for the day. Pritchett agreed (Raines, 1983, pp. 363–365).

While this move may have mystified some of King's detractors, King was clear about the focus of nonviolent action and its aim: to condemn the violent act and not the person. While in Birmingham King also deeply affected a Nazi-like sympathizer who bullied and beat King. He took the beating and then turned his attention to the sympathizer with compassion. McWhorter writes: "They were astounded to watch King become his assailant's protector. He held him solicitously and, as the audience began singing Movement songs, told him that their cause was just, that violence was self-demeaning, that "we're going to win." Then King introduced him to the crowd, as though he were a surprise guest. Roy James, a twenty-four-year-old native New Yorker who lived in an American Nazi Party dormitory in Arlington, Virginia, began to weep in King's embrace (Gladwell, 2013, p. 276, McWhorter, 2001, p. 277).

King believed that evil begins within. Therefore, hating the other one misses the most important step in nonviolence; the origin of evil lives within and can only be cured from within. According to Jung (1954),

> The inner voice is the voice of a fuller life, of a wider, more comprehensive consciousness ... What the inner voice whispers to us is something negative, if not evil. The inner voice ... makes us conscious of the evil from which the whole community is suffering, whether it be the nation or

the whole human race. But, it presents this evil in an individual form, so that one might at first suppose it to be only an individual characteristic (para. 318).

King's understanding of the origins of evil enabled him to endure tremendous suffering for the sake of his human family. His persistent refusal to hate brought an awareness of evil to the other, but also contributed to the eventual collapse of racist systems (if not to racist hearts) in the face of nonviolent scrutiny.

In the end, King would win anti-segregation rights for African Americans in Birmingham and later throughout the South, leading to the eventual passing of the Civil Rights Act of 1964. While the passing of this legislation did not immediately or permanently change the behaviors of the South, it shaped the desired spiritual ethos of the collective from which a new nonviolent ethic would emerge.

Nonviolent philosophy focuses on the protection of the spirit, the source and center of human experience. While the soul has a lifetime to unfold, its development can be impaired, sometimes arrested completely through the actions of other human beings. The practice of nonviolence protects the spirit by vowing nonviolence in response to the other. In Kingian nonviolence, the fourth tenet states: "The nonviolent resister is willing to accept violence if necessary, but never to inflict it" (1958, p. 92). Accepting violence requires tremendous humility, understanding, patience, persistence, practice, vision and abiding love of humankind to defeat violence and renunciate the instinctual urge to power within oneself.

During the Selma marches, demonstrators withstood tear gas, beatings, and whippings to induce shadow. Acceptance of suffering for the sake of the other activates the unconscious and brings to the surface the hatred in the oppressor. Voluntary suffering disorients the powers at hand, throwing the dictatorial equilibrium off balance, providing an opening heretofore inaccessible to the oppressor for a new awareness of their behavior. The oppressor can choose to look, or not. It was not uncommon for the demonstrators to pray for their oppressors, whether it be their jailors or the town's Sheriff Clark, their main antagonist. Suffering the aggressions of attackers was central to nonviolent training. Gandhi states that "given a just cause, capacity for endless suffering and avoidance of violence, victory is certain" (Kurlansky, 2006, p. 148). Nonviolence means accepting suffering for the sake of the other and the greater good.

King (1958) felt that there was much to learn about human nature in turning the other cheek. While blacks had been forced for centuries to be passive in the face of oppression, nonviolence offered a way to actively utilize passivity in service of autonomy. In this way, suffering for the sake of the other becomes transformative. Indeed, it very well may be that the archetypal constellation of nonviolence emerges through the vector of passivity in the split, fed by aggression and hatred, but enforced by a new urge to life, a psychic image, which finds its opening through a consciousness-infused passivity.

The fourth tenet provides a powerful intervention to the unconscious life of the oppressor, and offers a new way, for it reaches into the soul where reason cannot. Renunciation of violence reveals and potentially transforms the shadow of the oppressor. As Jung (1964/1970) states, "to confront a person with his shadow is to show him his own light" (para. 872).

King's fifth tenet states that "nonviolence avoids not only external violence but also internal violence of spirit" (1958, p. 92). Transforming violence in such a way requires understanding and accepting the human spirit as a sacred and unique form of expression of divine energy, whether one defines this energy as God, Brahman, or Jung's definition of the Self. Nonviolence is the practice of pursuing and procuring this energy. This tenet expresses the vital necessity of confronting and rooting out hatred as it threatens the fabric of the individual spirit and the collective soul. For King, love sits at the center of nonviolence, and that by projecting the "ethic of love to the center of our lives," one can "break the chain of hate" (King, 2010, p. xi). The force of nonviolence cuts through persona and ego making contact with shadow, bringing the other fully into view. Indeed, the other tends to be elusive and shapeshifting, determined by a cavalcade of factors defined by race, money, class, religion or political alliance, making the implementation of the ethic of nonviolence exceedingly challenging. However, the constellation of the archetypal experience of nonviolence emerges between self and other long before the conscious intent of nonviolence reaches the mind, body experience.

The political split in America has been ripening for decades now, the forces of violence threatening to rupture the current cultural fabric. The national division and vitriol has been no more evident than in the 2016 election of President Donald Trump and the months that have followed. Exhausted, browbeaten and traumatized by the political process of the 2016 elections, many Americans found themselves frustrated, angry, and some even filled with hatred for their opposing political parties by the time the mid-terms arrived in November 2018.

Voters were bombarded by emails, phone calls or personal visits from Democratic or Republican canvassers confirming voter registration as well as providing polling locations. Danny, a Democrat, had volunteered to canvass the neighborhood for his party for a few days leading up to the elections. Upon ringing the doorbell of one potential voter, Danny was greeted by the voter's husband: "Hello, my name is Danny, and I'm from the Democratic Party here to speak with Rita—is she home?" "Who are you?" growled the man hiding behind the screen door. Danny, a bit taken aback by his aggressiveness, gulped and swayed from one foot to the next. He quickly contemplated a clean getaway, and then ambivalently affirmed that he had come to check with Rita, the home's only registered Democrat, and offer assistance, if necessary, regarding voting poll locations.

Her husband, looking very menacing and disturbed, barked out a question which reflected his apparent disdain for his wife's political affiliation, "Are you a Democrat?" Danny, obviously understanding that he might be in trouble with his answer, began to stammer, but held his ground, "Hhhhmmm, yes, I'm a Democrat." "Well, I hate you people. You've done nothing but stir up trouble, you're ruining this country, and I'm sick of all of you. Get the hell outta here." In singular, dramatic fashion, the man pushed the screen door opened, forcing Danny to step back. He paused and took a breath. Feeling the vitriolic, political bile rising in his throat, he knew that he had stepped into an opportunity for political debate, and even violence. Indeed, "*these* were the *kinds* of people he reviled." He began to run his typical mind script: "Jesus, you won the election, *your* President is systematically dismantling climate change initiatives, economic trade agreements, immigration policies, tax codes ...!" Danny could feel the heat of his rage rising from his belly, spitfire, fast, his heart palpitating, his emotions threatening to spiral out of control. Yet, there was something about this man that was vulnerable and even, yes, frightened.

Despite his anger at feeling attacked, Danny decided to stop and check himself. He decided to stick to the script his political party gave him. Gathering his voice together, he began to speak calmly, concisely and democratically to the man; "I'm sorry for bothering you. I'm not here to talk about politics, or our party affiliations, it's clear that we have very different views. I get that. But I'm here just doing my job, making sure the right to vote is implemented for all those folks that are registered. I just thought I could assist Rita with information about her voting location if she hasn't done so already. He held his gaze as if to say, "I'm not one of those *kinds* of people." After a few moments, Danny felt a break in the tension, a flip into something bigger that flowed, eased up and into both of their bodies. Yes, it was a resolute surrender in the moment to something unknown but knowable between the two men, the residue of party affiliation giving way to human suffering. Reflexively, Danny stepped back while leaning in. The stranger receded into the house, shutting the door, but not before telling Danny that Rita wasn't home. Danny felt anger tinged with sadness at the unresolved situation and wondered to himself what it must be like for Rita and her partner to live together with different political party affiliations.

Danny walked to the next block, climbed into his car, and began reviewing the new section of the surrounding neighborhood map he needed to canvass. Startled by a knock on his window, Danny turned to see the stranger staring into his eyes. This time the glaze of fiery hatred had receded, replaced by a sheepish vulnerability. He looked so small. Danny rolled his window down. Rita's husband states, "I'm so glad I found you. Uhm. I just wanted to apologize for my attitude back there. I was totally outa line. I don't know what came over me, but I had no right to speak to you that way."

Danny's body drained of anxiety, as his feelings of relief, surprise and gratitude flooded throughout his body. Overcome by his neighbor's courage and humility. He got out of the car and shook the real man's hand.

> Thank so much for this. I'm so touched you came and found me, and I'm so glad to meet you. We're all going through a hard time right now. It's been so rough, but you've made my day. Thank you, again.

After talking for a few more minutes, they parted ways, Danny deeply touched by the humility of a stranger. He then understood how Rita and her partner bridged their differences. But the mystery of the alchemy that gets one to a place of humility and strength was awe-inspiring for Danny. He could not formulate the words for the compassion-fused experience he had with this stranger and his desire to overcome bitterness and hatred—the brief exchange set in motion an alchemical process touched by *Agape*, driven by a mutual desire for peace in both people. The split within the political culture and community momentarily disrupted the negative political split through the nonviolent actions of both men. Danny had to withdraw his projection onto Republicans that they are incapable of self-reflection, while his neighbor had to confront within himself a belief that all Democrats are troublemakers and elitists.

Something important happened between Danny and his neighbor in the encounter before election day. The union reached down and into the personal and communal realms of existence. Through this union, the divine was accessed, and love or *Agape* was experienced. Indeed, the right to vote is not just about the act of voting but is symbolic of the individual's existential struggle for freedom and meaning which exists somewhere between self and other, individual and community. According to King:

> The Holy Spirit is the continuing community creating reality that moves through history. He who works against community is working against the whole of creation. Therefore, if I respond to hate with a reciprocal hate I do nothing but intensify the cleavage in broken community. I can only close the gap in broken community by meeting hate with love. (1958, p. 94)

Through nonviolence, the individual is cleaved to community, the personality becoming manifest. No one can individuate without the other.

King's sixth tenet states "Nonviolence is based on the conviction that the universe is on the side of justice" (1958, p. 95). King's faith in God forms the sixth tenet. He believed that faith enabled one to work for the betterment of his brother and sister and to withstand persecution and suffering for the sake of the other. For King, the relationship between God and human was ultimately a creative one, working toward a singular purpose of spiritual wholeness. It could be argued that King's notion of a harmonious cosmos which serves a just purpose is an idealized notion; however, King was certain and steadfast in his beliefs. The notion of justice guided him through the darkest of times:

> There are certain spiritual experiences that we continue to have, that cannot be explained with materialistic notions. One knows deep down within there is something in the very structure of the cosmos that will ultimately bring about fulfillment and the triumph of that which is right. And this is the only thing that can keep one going in difficult times. (Garrow, 1986, p. 290)

King believed that beneath the complexities of life there existed a spiritual, cosmic superstructure which was ever changing yet organized. The difficulty of King's statement is that he assumes justice has an outcome that is "right." As a Christian, this implies a morality based on right vs. wrong. In the world of psyche; however, morality emerges not from an ego-oriented consciousness, but from the transcendent function, or the relationship between the conscious and unconscious realms. The way of the third (an aspect of psychic wholeness), or justice, will emerge through a form of consciousness determined by the Self and its degree of manifestation in both parties.

References

Ajgaonkar, S. M. (1995). *Mahatma A Golden Treasury of Wisdom - Thoughts & Glimpses of Life*. Mumbai:Hripra Publication.

considerthedog.com. (2018, July 15). Retrieved from http://considerthedog.com: https://youtu.be/_WLPSncgbf0.

Gandhi, M. (1962). *The Essential Gandhi: An Anthology of His Writings on Life, Work, and Ideas*. New York: Vintage Books.

Garrow, D. (1986). *Bearing the Cross*. New York: Perennial Classics.

Ghaemi, N. (2011). *A First-Rate Madness*. London: Penguin Books.

Gladwell, Malcolm (2013). *David and Goliath: Underdogs, Misfits and the Art of Battling Giants*. New York: Little, Brown and Company.

Haga, K. (2015, January 20). Shut it Down: Reclaiming the Radical Legacy of Dr. Martin Luther King, Jr. Retrieved from *Buddhistpeacefellowship.org*: http://www.buddhistpeacefellowship.org/shut-it-down-reclaim-the-legacy/.

Hartford, B. (2004/1963). http://www.crmvet.org/info/nv1.htm. Retrieved from https://www.crmvet.org/:https://www.crmvet.org/info/nv1.htm.

Hillman, J. (2004). *A Terrible Love of War*. New York: Penguin Press.

Jung, C. (1954). *The Collected Works of C.G. Jung, The Development of the Personality*, Volume 17 (W. McGuire, ed.). Princeton: Princeton University Press.

Jung, C. (1964/1970). *The Collected Works of C.G. Jung: Civilization in Transition*, Volume 10. Princeton: Princeton University Press.

King J., Martin Luther (1958). *Stride Toward Freedom: The Montgomery Story*. Boston: Beacon Press.

King, J., Martin Luther (2010). *Strength to Love*. Minneapolis: Fortress Press.

Kunhardt, P. (Director). (2018). *King in the Wilderness* [Motion Picture].

Kurlansky, M. (2006). *Nonviolence: the History of a Dangerous Idea*. New York: Random House.

McWhorter, D. (2001). *Carry Me Home Birmingham, Alabama The Climactic Battle of the Civil Rights Revolution*. New York: Simon & Schuster.

Petri, F. (Summer 2014). Gandhi, Jung and Nonviolence Today The Relevance of the Feminine in the Network Society. *IIC Quarterly*, 41(1), 7–18.

Raines, H. (1983). *My Soul is Rested: The Story of the Civil Rights Movement in the Deep South*. New York: Penguin.

Samuels, A. (1985). *Jung And The Post Jungians*. London, New York: Routledge.

WGBH (Director). (2019). *The Violence Paradox* [Motion Picture].

Wink, W. (2000). *Peace is the Way Writings on Nonviolence from the fellowship of Reconciliation*. Maryknoll: Orbis Books.

Chapter 5

Why we march

A march is significant as an initiatory experience in cultural development. As part of the human narrative, the mass march signals disunion between a culture's ideals and values and its preservation of them. The march is a call by the people to restore moral order within a culture that has gone astray, or more deeply, a demand for spiritual reconciliation with the forces of oppression which threaten the lives of the individuals within a community or the culture at large. The march joins the voices of the one to the many; it is a distress call signaling labor pains in development; a new trajectory in the "we-ness" of a nation. The image of the dream is already in the pipeline of the collective unconscious, but it will not be birthed into a new way of life until violent, destructive, collective energies are mediated through much suffering and nonviolent activism. Nature includes both violence and nonviolence, whose unique relationship performs an alchemical symphony of upheaval followed by quiescence, leaving in its wake a new image of a natural order.

The march provides the crucible in which violent communal forces can be catalyzed into new psychic life. This process begins within the individual and ends within the community, the march itself an orchestration of the collective's migratory instincts urging the herd into action. Through the march, members of the collective unconsciously link up and synchronistically come together in a collective movement defined by a similar purpose.

It is the eve of my fifty-eighth birthday, January 17, 2017. After a long day of work and a teeth-grinding hour of national news, I fall into bed, anticipating with excitement my upcoming weekend. I am certain it will be a life-changing experience. As my body is lulled into sleep, the dream images appear, until, suddenly, I am jarred into a semiconscious state, my body moving to the rhythm of the bed. The swaying morphs into shaking, and then a rumbling sensation unfolds around me. My nerve endings ignite like a forest fire ripping through my body sounding the alarm. My memory banks rip open. I know this feeling. It is an earthquake and a big one. I must find shelter—a doorway or a bathtub—or run outside, if possible. I run into my garage as the earthquake begins to roar—a lucid dream somewhere on the edge between here and there. I have always been fascinated by these kinds of dreams: a state of half waking and half-sleeping existence, an alternate reality, an opening perhaps to somewhere and something greater than myself.

The quake is in full rhythm now: heaving, sighing, slamming, shaking, heaving, sighing, slamming, shaking. I look back at the garage doors knocked off their hinges, lying cockeyed, gawking at me. After what feels like an eternity, the rocking begins to subside. As I crawl out from under the quake's grip, I am left deeply shaken and physically anxious. As I lie in bed, attempting to calm my breathing, I persuade my mind's eye to focus on the images of the dream when, suddenly, the meaning hits me with the force of the earthquake.

The dream is prospective, for in two days, I will be heading to Washington DC for an event that will draw millions more people than anticipated. It will be a collective experience celebrated throughout American cities and across the globe. The earth's heaving song is the rhythmic sound of millions of people marching around the world for human rights. The broken garage doors symbolize the end of my separation from the world and heralding a fusion with a collective experience. The division between the inside and outside worlds has shifted, exposing me to the collective unconscious. Maybe the dream indicates the dawning of a new attitude, not just for me but for the collective as well.

I could not know at the time that the Women's March of January 2017 would usher in a new civil activism within America, giving birth to multiple movements addressing an historical, hypocrisy-laced oppression in America defined by misogyny and racism. The president's unwitting invitation to millions of America's women would be answered by people across the globe, and the party favors of pink pussy hats would be a pronouncement of a new birthday for the American female politician.

The march that formed in response to the recent election of Donald Trump gathered a storm cloud of fury in many women and fellow Americans who felt that the nation's new president was threatening our democratic values. Moreover, the protests and marches globally have reflected a moral crisis within the American soul in general and the body politic specific to Donald Trump and his administration's policies, which threaten the headway that women have made in recent generations and promote the reversal of the few sociopolitical gains achieved. However, Trump is not solely the problem, but rather the manifestation of an age-old problem, the oppressive, misogyny-infused atmosphere in Washington politics which consistently denies women their right to participate in a life based on the very doctrines and laws passed addressing freedom for all Americans.

Today's women are fed up with the retractions of promises made by political leaders and are determined, this time, to change it. Trump has become a lightning rod for women, who are not going to lose the small gains which they have strived for centuries to acquire. It is a touchy thing, the march. Activism must titrate and utilize rage appropriately, injecting it with nonviolent consciousness. The hundreds of thousands of women gathered in Washington have to act nonviolently, refusing to give others reason to, once again, label us as uncontrolled hysterics. In *Good and Mad: The Revolutionary Power of Women's Anger*, writer and journalist Rebecca Traister (2018) speaks to the delicate nature of rage-taming through nonviolent activism:

> Social movements are necessarily about challenging social controls. This is what social change is built on, and what America's politics themselves are built on … [But] insurrections don't always work; in fact, they don't *often* work, in part … because the rage that that fuels them has the power to burn them. Which is just part of what makes them scary; the other thing that makes them scary is that they are designed to destabilize power structures, often the ones that have been abusive, but are nonetheless the only ones we've got. (p. 40)

Nonviolent activism can keep the rage from becoming the destructive insurrection that Traister describes. Through our female nature women can utilize the energy of coming together to mobilize new ideas while breaking down old barriers. Indeed, the march itself was but a physical manifestation of collective psychological forces rising up and into consciousness and being delivered to the front steps of the White House the day after Trump's inauguration, January 21, 2017, by a conflagration of pink-pussy-capped women.

The morning of the march brought an excitement that the biting cold could not deter. I joined the hundreds of thousands of women in downtown Washington, where a stage formed the central point of the crucible from which the alchemical flow of the march occurred. Propping myself up on a steel barrier, all I could see was a sea of pink hats expanding from the Native American Museum over to the Capitol in one direction, and to the Washington Monument in another—all of this birthed from the call of the one to the many.

As the day unfolded, Martin Luther King's name became a prominent force delivered by the speakers and absorbed by the crowd. As I gazed out at the expanse of women, my mind drifted back to the first march on Washington 1963.

The marchers stood patiently listening to the rally that continued for over four hours. As the afternoon developed, they began to get restless. Chants of "March! March! March!" were spawned sporadically throughout the multitudes. At one point, while waiting for the march to start, the compression and heat of all the bodies began to take hold within the crowd. Agitation spread, and a restlessness due to the palpable and frightening feeling of compression began to take shape, threatening to pop. A wave of claustrophobia spilled into my bowels, as I fought the urge to heave. The tension in the air was electric; everyone wanted to move, to give birth to collective protest. At once, I realized that the threat of a stampede was genuine. It suddenly became clear that the march was frozen, the route clogged all the way to the capital, hundreds of thousands of people jammed together, immobile.

As if on cue, the tension broke, a collective sigh was released, as marchers began to spill into the surrounding streets, seeking any viaduct they could find to start their march. The pushing and heaving gave way to a flowing river of pink pussy hats, banners, and posters. People chanted, sang, or walked in silence, holding signs, candles, and each other. They hung from overpasses and dangled out of windows. I heard a symphony of chants blending and at times clashing: "Hey hey, ho ho, Donald Trump has got to go!" "What do you want? Freedom!" "When do we want it? Now!" "We will not be silenced!" The march felt majestic, infused with a history of the nation and all the marches before it.

The serpentine flow, writhing its way to some unknown destination, was electrifying. I was being drawn into a collective spiritual unfolding, while simultaneously experiencing a return to something fundamental, tribal—a sense of identity only experienced in a group. While marching, I wondered about all the revolutions before me that effected change, building upon a singular shared ideal, a vision so strong that suffering and the sacrifice of life itself became secondary to the dream. At that moment, I wished that I knew what others had dreamt before the march. A dream within the collective unconscious, carried within the psyches of the marchers, had been unleashed. We could not know at the time what our march would produce, but the midterm elections of 2018 were proof of the power of the dream.

In the fall of 2018, the midterm elections would spark an awakening within the political system that ushered a record number of 117 women into the Washington political system. The Associated Press reported,

> The Election Day gains by women were the capstone on a midterm election that has been defined by the energy of women, both on the political left and right. Women not only ran for office at an unprecedented rate, several knocked off white male incumbents during their party primaries. They mobilized on the grassroots level and played larger roles as donors than in previous election cycles. (Summers and Mulvihill, 2018, para. 5)

Women's determination to call out the corruption within the misogynistic political system and the nation at large had begun with a dream.

It is from the dream that the wellspring of life flows and ebbs, carrying with it individual and collective material, reflecting the psychic position of the dreamer. The dream contains a storehouse of knowledge that mediates one's outer and inner worlds, augmenting or compensating for the dreamer's position and pointing the way toward a more balanced position by revealing a different, sometimes opposite, point of view to consciousness.

The dream points the way to individuation, through the guiding Self, or the archetypal Self, which is to be viewed as a source and director of the individuation drive ... as well as the source and director of life events and of dream material, both providing invaluable metaphoric/allegoric and symbolic messages which aid the individuation process to those who learn to read them. (Whitmont and Perera, 1989, p. 18)

Examining one of Jung's dreams points the way to understanding how the cross-pollination of dreams between the individual and culture affects the development of each.

In December 1937, when Jung traveled to India, he experienced powerful dreams while struggling to recover from a bout of amoebic dysentery (Bair, 2003, p. 428). Based on Jung's report of a particularly powerful dream about his search for the Holy Grail, biographer Deirdre Bair (2003) discusses Jung's experience:

In the hospital, he slipped in and out of drugged sleep, having dreams he "could not understand at all." They all had one thing in common, and in his periods of lucidity, he realized that each centered around a different image of the Holy Grail. He was either on a quest to recover it for a group of unknown supplicants or charged by people he knew to bring it back to where they thought it belonged. In one of the dreams he was able to remember most completely, he described himself as being in India but high above the subcontinent and looking down on an island shaped like England. Where Cornwall should have been, there was a promontory with a medieval castle where he saw himself and various Psychological Club members, both men and women, "*sight-seeing.*" He entered the castle through the dungeon where he could look skyward in an enormous tower. An iron gate and stone staircase led to a large hall, where a sign informed visitors that the Holy Grail would be celebrated. Jung was "impressed," but his companions were not. The situation changed, and although he was still with the club members, they were all men. The group began to march in another direction, still intent on attending the Grail celebration. They were now out in the countryside and marched all day until, exhausted, they came to a body of water that cut the island in two. "How do we go on?" Jung asked himself in his dream. "Everything is deserted and bleak. Goodness, what to do?" As there was "no boat, no bridge, no street at all," he knew he had to swim across: "I knew one thing for sure: I have to reach that Grail." At that point he awakened, but the dream remained for the rest of his life one of his "most powerful dream impressions." (pp. 428–429)

Jung's dream connects the individual to the culture and the collective unconscious, the dream revealing the multiple and variant geological formations of the human psyche. Jung is in the throes of a calling to a higher order within himself and within the group of men and women who are *sight-seeing* (seekers and seers of consciousness). However, as the women fall away, Jung is chosen or called to carry something that doesn't interest the others. Indeed, in his waking life, this task burdened Jung, both professionally and personally, yet, he knew that his great calling was to deliver his psychological theory of the archetypal Self to the world.

At one point in the dream, Jung finds himself on a journey with the men of the group as they march for days, seeking the Grail celebration. The march is the essential journey of seeking spiritual wholeness through the acquisition of a life oriented toward making the unconscious conscious; however, a conscious life requires the attainment of many things. Of vital importance is one's ability to wrestle with inner demons, working consciously to accept them and tame their destructiveness. Jung's shadow appears in the image of the many men (psychic fragments) who must unify for a confrontation with the split forces of his psyche. This would require Jung to work through his complexes with women (who disappear in the dream), for the dream also reflects Jung's anima complex, or his search to recover the wounded feminine within.

When Jung comes to the body of water that divides the land, he has encountered his psychological split, which must be healed in the discovery of the Grail. Jung's initial uncertainty and his decision to swim across *are* the solution. Wrestling with his shadow elements, getting in the bath with them, *is* the Grail path. Bair (2003) continues:

> Jung described individuation as "a mystery one will never understand." To find it was a "lonely search" perhaps akin to the "process of dying," for one had to give oneself "over to the impersonal" in order to seek it. "Only few could bear such a search," he thought, attributing these curious, unfocused thoughts and images to the "the distance from Europe, the completely different surroundings" in which he found himself in India. He thought he may have had such dreams there because his overall question was how and why the evil he encountered in India was "not a moral dimension," but rather "supported by an honest profession of divine power." (p. 429)

Jung's marching dream not only reveals his feminine complex, but India's feminine wound and subsequent emancipation from oppressive British Rule (1757–1947) through Gandhi's pioneering feminine based revolution. The split land in the dream represents the split between India and Pakistan.

A mere seven years earlier, Gandhi initiated India's spiritual genesis with the infamous twenty-six-mile Salt March (1930), an act of civil disobedience protesting the high salt tax imposed by British authorities. With Gandhi's guidance, India would win her freedom in 1947. Beginning with this march, Gandhi's path toward peace awakened and unified millions of people through the alchemy of nonviolent activism. Indeed, in his dream, Jung's inner condition met with the outer circumstances of the culture in the image of the demonstration. In analyzing the dream, one could ponder the imprint of the cultural pattern on Jung's psyche and from whence it originated. The dream addresses a deeply mystical layer of existence, which Jung called the Self revealed through archetypal patterns connecting individuals to something greater than themselves, transgenerationally and beyond. In his book *Call Me by My True Names*, Buddhist monk Thich Nhat Hanh (1999), describes this phenomenon beautifully: "If you touch deeply the historical dimension, you find yourself in the ultimate dimension; If you touch the ultimate dimension, you have not left the historical dimension" (front face). In his book, *Depth Psychology and a New Ethic*, Jungian analyst Erich Neumann (1969/1990) poses that the connection between the individual and the collective is closer than we imagine and indicates that the solution to cultural problems may, indeed, lie within the individual:

> Both the problem and the level at which the solution emerges are manifested in the individual; both, however, have their roots in the collective. It is precisely this that makes the experience of the individual so significant. What happens in him is typical of the total situation, and the creative stirrings which enable him to find his own solutions and salvation are the initial stages of the future values and symbols of the collective. (pp. 29–30)

The march is a mythological narrative formed from the bones of an ageless story, instinctively repeated throughout history, unifying the individual to the collective through a shared dream. Jungian analyst Marie-Louise von Franz in her book *Archetypal Dimensions of the Psyche*, agrees with Neumann's idea that the individual and collective psyches are closely linked, and finds this fusion in the myth-making process of the culture: "The myths make clear, among other things, the idea that humanity originally had a collective soul: psychically, all people were a unity" (Franz, 1994, p. 254). The march is a collective dream coming into being through an unconscious unifying factor, the Self—that unknowable essence within all human beings that historically, experientially, and spiritually binds us together.

Archetypal patterns of individuation appear throughout history, and many begin with a march. Whether it be King guiding his people out of a wilderness of oppression and slavery, or Moses's pilgrimage leading his people to the promised land, the march brings together a chosen, or self-selected group of people reflective of a collective attitude, who commit themselves to the process of transforming their culture. The group becomes the carrier of something greater than its individual members as it seeks reconciliation with forces in culture that have fallen short of a collectively expressed ideal. Neumann (1969/1990) explains,

The future of the collective lives in the present of the individual, hard pressed as he is by his problems—which can, in fact, be regarded as the organs of this collective. The sensitive, psychically disturbed and creative people are always the forerunners. Their enhanced permeability by the contents of the collective unconscious, the deep layer which determines the history of happenings in the group, makes them receptive to emerging new contents of which the collective is not yet aware. But these are the people for whom problems become insistent in their personal lives a hundred years or more before the collective has woken up to their existence. (p. 30)

Our national suffering unifies us through the marginalized citizenry whose self-chosen few openly grieve and rebel together through the march, demanding a reconciliation for their oppression. Not only in rebellion do they suffer, but through empathy, compassion, and *agape*, they join together to heal and forge a future filled with the altruistic image of *agape*-infused peace. Yet, they suffer for they carry the cultural wound at large.

Before the marches in Selma, the largest civil rights gathering in American history occurred during the March on Washington, August 28, 1963, when an estimated 250,000 people gathered on the mall to protest the civil injustices being committed against the disenfranchised and to support the Kennedy administration's passing of the Civil Rights Act, which was being negotiated within Congress (Clayborne Carson, 2001, p. 75). The idea for the march was the result of a dream born twenty years before its manifestation as the dream child of A. Philip Randolph, an African American activist (National Park Service, 2017). Organized by Bayard Rustin, the demonstration began with a mile-long march ending on the mall with a series of speeches, culminating with King's infamous "I Have a Dream" speech. Indeed, the march on Washington was a dream iterating King's (2001) vision for a free America, still unfolding today:

I say to you today, my friends, so even though we face the difficulties of today and tomorrow, I still have a dream. It is a dream deeply rooted in the American Dream ... I have a dream that one day this nation will rise up and live out the true meaning of its creed: "We hold these truths to be self-evident, that all men are created equal." ... I have a dream that my four little children will one day live in a nation where they will not be judged by the color of their skin but by the content of their character. I have a dream today. I have a dream that one day down in Alabama, with its vicious racists, with its governor having his lips dripping with the words of 'interposition' and 'nullification,' one day right there in Alabama little black boys and black girls will be able to join hands with the little white boys and white girls as sisters and brothers. I have a dream today. (p. 85)

King's speech was archetypal containing images past, present, and future—bringing together a timeless motif of a dream born from the millions and delivered by the one.

A mere two years later, King would carry to Selma the dream birthed in Washington and, there, begin to change the nation, once again through the march. Just as the March on Washington of 1963 culminated with the passing of the Civil Rights Act of 1964, the Selma marches would bear the gift of the Voting Rights Act of 1965. The Women's March on Washington of 2017, now the largest in American history, carried the seeds of King's dream speech, this time calling for the reconciliation of racial and feminine oppression becoming the new civil rights movement, the human rights movement. The dream for the march which began on the internet, another viaduct to the collective unconscious, gave birth to a sociopolitical movement designed to inject the feminine into a patriarchate, corrupted by power.

Since the American Presidential election of 2016, protests have increased across the country, almost all taking shape through social media. The Women's March of 2017 was followed by the #metoo movement, #timesup, #blacklivesmatter, #nobannowall, and #marchforourlives campaigns. These mass movements reflect the presence of a cultural neurosis whereby a group of individuals that make up part of the collective is at odds with the cultural values and morals held therein. These individuals are usually a marginalized part of culture who carry the shadow projections, or cast off, denied aspects of the collective identity (Neumann,1969/1990, p. 52). These are the exiled seeking a new home. The call to march is the demand for reconciliation and recognition of the marginalized.

The culture's individuation begins with the uprising through the marginalized who carry the projections of the suppressed aspects of the collective personality, seeking consciousness. According to Neumann (1969/1990):

> Inside a nation, the aliens who provide the objects for this projection are the minorities; if these are of a different racial or ethnological complexion or, better still, of a different colour, their suitability for this purpose is particularly obvious. This psychological problem of the minorities is to be found with the religious, national, racial and social variations; it is, however, symptomatic, in every case of a split in the structure of the collective. (p. 52)

The archetypal experience of democracy in America is partially defined by a lineage of marches that carry within their numbers the marginalized, who signify the moral problem of their time but who also carry the solution. According to Neumann, the individual is to the collective as the wheat is to the chaff, indicating that the answers to the collective's problems also lies within the individual:

The connection between the problems of the individual and those of the collective is far closer than is generally realized. We are still by no means always aware of the 'totality constellation' by virtue of which each single individual is an organ of the collective, whose common inner structure he bears in his collective unconscious. In this structure, the collective is no abstraction but the unity of all the individuals in which it is represented. (p. 31)

Mass demonstrations carry within their folds the seeds to collective moral reconciliation which begins with the uprising; each individual carrying an aspect of the collective unconscious, which often finds its unique expression through a collective experience. Nonviolent activism is the fulcrum that forces a rectification of injustice upon the community through more than mirror gazing, for it also germinates a new cultural ethic. The new ethic is the "development and differentiation within the old ethic, confined at present to those uncommon individuals, who driven by unavoidable conflicts of duty, endeavour to bring the conscious and the unconscious into responsible relationship" (Neumann, 1969/1990, p. 15). Where the old ethic consists of the ego's relationship to consciousness, the new ethic is an attitude of ego to conscious and unconscious. Collective movement from the old to the new ethic requires shadow integration, on both individual and collective levels. During the civil rights movement, King, like Moses and Gandhi before him, was the individual, the one voice to bridge the collective dream to reality and although the current human rights movement is burgeoning, no one leader has emerged to unify the collective.

Today, across the globe, immigrants are on the move, seeking freedom from oppressive conditions. Venezuela, Mexico, and Syria are but a few countries whose marginalized have become mobilized and pour across the borders of their neighboring countries. Currently, mass exodus is occurring in Venezuela, with millions of its citizens becoming refugees. Reacting to the "socialist revolution" launched by the late president Hugo Chávez in 1999, the exodus of Venezuelans "turned into a flood as living conditions … [became] ever more dire—from hyperinflation to acute shortages of food and medicine to one of the worst homicide rates in the world" (Tegel, 2017, para. 4).

According to a 2018 report by the International Rescue Committee (IRC), an international humanitarian crisis response agency, "in the face of the unprecedented collapse of the country's economy and health systems," up to 3 million Venezuelans had left the country since 2015, with 1 million settling in Colombia. With the deepening crisis in Venezuela, the United Nations estimated that by the end of 2019, over 5 million refugees would "be displaced, with 2 million expected in Colombia alone—eclipsing the Syrian refugee crisis" (para. 8).

As of 2017, over 5 million refugees have fled Syria due to civil war, and in Myanmar, over 700,00 refugees have fled the country since 2017

(World Vision, 2019). The world order is on the move, leaving a large swath of populations alienated from their cultures and left vulnerable to disease, starvation, and homelessness. Military rebellions, civil wars, and tyrannical leaders—stripping citizens of civil rights, freedom, and hope— feed these mass escapes.

Moses and King carried the dream, a new vision of freedom, for their people. They both held legacies which enabled them to understand the trans-generational spiritual crisis at hand as well as exercise their capacity to hold collective suffering and serve as a mediating force of nature for the people. They were the hermetic healers and heroes of their time, sharing legacies, separated by centuries, fused in a mythological narrative of individuation.

Although the march may be a powerful experience, the past century's initiation is only the beginning, and even the effort of people like King and Gandhi may not be enough. African Americans still suffer from abject pov-erty, neglect, and cultural deprivation. Anti-Semitism is globally on the rise, and millions of people are transmigrating due to poverty and war. Soon, due to global warming, even millions more will be displaced due to rising water levels, drought and flooding.

The path of personal and collective individuation is complex, a pattern influenced by violence and war, with the experience of peace and conscious-ness only momentarily wrenched from the grip of the experience through nonviolence. Examining the archetypal patterns of nonviolent activism may provide access to human's capacity to cultivate altruism and harmony and may very well be the ultimate human calling of our time. Much work is to be done on an individual basis, however, for the procurement of a collective dream. The march points towards the moral problem while procuring a dream still to be realized. Further investigation of the Selma marches sheds light on the process of the development of a new ethic.

References

Bair, D. (2003). *Jung: A Biography.* Boston, New York, London: Little Brown and Company.

Clayborne Carson, K. S. (2001). *A Call to Conscience: the Landmark Speeches of Dr. Martin Luther King, Jr.* New York: Time Warner Book Group.

Franz, M.-L. v. (1994). *Archetypal Dimensions of the Psyche.* Boston: Shambala.

Hanh, T. N. (1999). *Call Me By My True Names.* Berkley: Parallax Press. https://www. aol.com. (2018, November 08). Retrieved from https://www.aol.com:https://www. aol.com/article/news/2018/11/07/divisive-trump-era-ushers-record-number-of-women-into-house/23582604/https://www.rescue.org/press-release/holiday-season-approaches-irc-voice-morena-baccarin-calls-support-venezuelan-refugees. (2018, December 21).

National Park Service. (2017). A. Philip Randolph. Retrieved from https://www.nps. gov/people./a-phillip-randolph.htm.

Neumann, E. (1969/1990). *Depth Psychology and a New Ethic.* Boston: Shambala Publications.

Summers, J., and Mulvihill, G. (2018, November 7). Divisive Trump Era Ushers Record Number of Women Into House. *AP News*. Retrieved from https://www.ap news.com/e88c914572824a9dadd4d080a459f6cb.

Tegel, S. (2017, December 14). Flood of Venezuelans are Fleeing Depressed Country. Here's Where They're Seeking Refuge, *USA Today*. Retrieved from https://www.usa today.com/story/news/world/2017/12/14/flood-venezuelans-fleeing-their-depressed-country/941463001/.

Traister, R. (2018). *Good and Mad: The Revolutionary Power of Women's Anger*. New York: Simon and Schuster.

Whitmont, E. C. and Perera, S. B. (1989). *Dreams the Portal to the Source*. New York: Routledge.

World Vision (2019). Syrian Refugee Crisis. Facts, FAQS and How to Help. Retrieved from https://www.worldvision.org/refugees-news-stories/syrian-refugee-crisis-facts.

Chapter 6

The trickster

The demonstrations had begun to take hold in the nation's psyche by the time February 1965 had rolled around. A good month of days had peeled themselves from the calendar since the start of the Selma campaign for voting rights, and by now, the marchers and the town's notable law enforcement officials had established a well-worn path around and into each other. Indeed, King and his lieutenants were master strategists and tricksters who drew the town's officials into their honey trap with predictable frequency.

With the precision of a finely tuned marching band, the demonstrators' nonviolent presence provoked a series of unconscious racist enactments that laid bare an unchecked immorality which had deeply infected the attitudes of civilians as well as many law enforcement officials. The media was masterfully playing into the hands of the tricksters and their foxlike ways as well. National news outlets showed up in Selma in January and with riveting frequency, filmed outbreaks of aggression by the town's officials, particularly the violent tantrums of the town's sheriff, James Clark. Clark's prickly temperament and short fuse was captured on grainy black and white film and preserved in the Public Broadcasting System's civil rights series, *Eyes on the Prize* (DeVinney, 1987).

Episode six of *Eyes on the Prize* (DeVinney, 1987) features a particularly cold and rainy day in February when Reverend C. T. Vivien leads the marchers to the courthouse for another day of mischief and nonviolent protest. Vivien, a charismatic powerhouse of a minister and key leader in the Southern Christian Leadership Conference, stands with the demonstrators outside of the Dallas County Courthouse facing off with the Sheriff. Clark, a burly deep-throated doppelganger of the openly racist Bull Connor from Birmingham, stands above the marchers on the steps of the courthouse, looking down at Vivien. Vivien, not to be deterred, speaks forcefully to Clark but more pointedly to the deputies who report to Clark:

> We want you to know, gentlemen, that every one of you, we know your badge numbers and we know your names ... But believe me, there were those that followed Hitler like you're following blindly this sheriff Clark,

who didn't think their day would come that (they) were also pulled into the courtrooms and they were also given their death sentences. You're not this bad of a racist, but you're racist in the same way Hitler was a racist, and you're blindly following a man that's leading you down a road that's going to bring you into a federal court, for this is not a local problem, gentlemen. This is a national problem. You can't keep anyone in the United States from voting without hurting the rights of all other citizens. Democracy is built on this! (1987, 11:30)

Clark begins swatting his billy club at the marchers as if to fend off flies from his afternoon lunch. By the time Vivien finishes his impassioned rant, he brings the sheriff to full froth, who then systematically begins poking and shoving the marchers from the courthouse steps, finally knocking Vivien to the ground. In this episode of the series, Clark would later state that he did not recall hitting Vivien. Vivien, pulling himself up from the sidewalk and brushing himself off, might as well have looked directly into the news cameras and winked. Once again, the trickster had pulled one over on the old fox. But Vivien's indignation and determination to break down the racist voting institutions in the South was not to be taken lightly; the grief was bone deep.

Tricksters are often charmers and masterful manipulators, albeit mostly unconsciously, displaying an uncanny capacity to bend seamlessly the will of others their way. They slip through the knot of consequence, disappearing in a flash and leaving the other feeling hoodwinked, as if something has been taken by sleight of hand, when in fact, it usually has. The question is what has been taken (or given) in this theft. Indeed, at the root of the trickster archetype is stealth; the ability to deliver oneself into a situation and change up the pattern of reality so quickly and forcefully that the magician's feat can be experienced only through a veil of confusion that leaves one feeling fundamentally altered but not quite knowing how or why.

The archetype of the trickster is mythologically based. In fact, most cultures have some aspect of the trickster within their mythological narrative. For Native Americans, the coyote is the symbol of the trickster, whereas in Hindu mythology, the trickster appears as the deity Krishna. Indeed, like the playful child, the trickster appears to turn one's world upside down, challenging the rules of the adult world and realigning morals and values which may have gone amuck.

According to Lewis Hyde (1998), in his book *Trickster Makes the World Mischief, Myth and Art*, Trickster is the master of boundaries, crossed over, or created in an effort to "get life going again" (p. 7). Getting life going involves the stirring up of emotion, sometimes violently in order to create order from chaos, or to dissolve order altogether. When trickster "becomes the messenger of the gods it's as if he has been enlisted to solve a problem he himself created. In a case like that, boundary creation and boundary crossing are related to one another, and the best way to describe trickster is to say simply that the boundary is where he will be found—sometimes drawing the line, sometimes crossing it, sometimes erasing it or moving it, but always there, the god of the threshold in all its forms (pp. 7–8). King and the protestors can easily be recognized as the manipulators of boundaries for very good reason, because through their nonviolent activism, they *revealed* the true face of racism in the South. And as Hyde points out trickster "brings to the surface a distinction previously hidden from sight" (p. 7).

It is from Hermes that the trickster gets its behavioral DNA. Living on the edge of naughtiness and avoidance of condemnation are essential traits of the trickster's nature. Trickster behavior can infuriate, enliven, endear, and even repel; however, the archetypal pattern of the trickster is deeply complex and profound, for the trickster has the capacity to transform nations, often not without wreaking tremendous havoc. Tricksters appear in situations that would otherwise seem impossible to change. They inadvertently shift the paradigm by metaphorically entering through the back door, because coming through the front is far too dangerous. Indeed, the presence of the trickster can feel as if there is a game of psychological hide-and-go-seek going on, the essence of something tangible illusively escaping the grip of consciousness.

The nature of the trickster can be found in the Greek myth *Homeric Hymn to Hermes*. At the opening of the myth Hermes, the infant, steals cattle from his brother Apollo, perhaps because he is jealous of Apollo's wealth. Maybe Hermes also senses something fishy or off-kilter that he wants to set straight. The question Hermes seems to address in the theft is "Why does Apollo get the riches and not me?" This tale of Hermes's stealing is not about the immorality in the act but rather points to the ethical impropriety of Apollo having more, and Hermes's wishes to call out the disjunction in the haves and have-nots. As Norman O. Brown (1947) relates in his book *Hermes the Thief*, "Hermes is considered the 'hero of stealthy appropriation". (p. 7)

But tricksters are not just mythological or fictional storybook characters found in legend and song. Trickster leaders have shaped civilizations, guided nations, and played an incremental role in developing the necessary dialogue for cultural bridge building. The lives of P. T. Barnum, Frederick Douglas, Winston Churchill, Lyndon Johnson, Bill Clinton, Mahatma Gandhi, Carl Jung, Sigmund Freud, John F. Kennedy, J. Edgar Hoover, Nancy Pelosi and Martin Luther King, Jr., to name a few, aptly demonstrate the diverse nature of the inner trickster and the vast cultural transformation that their lives induced and informed. Tricksters can heal collective wounds, stir up the status quo, and withstand the blowback from opposing cultural forces, often for the sake of a new moral order. Hyde (1998) poignantly describes the effects of trickster nature, emphasizing the influence the trickster has on the other:

> What tricksters quite regularly do is create lively talk where there has been silence, or where speech has been prohibited. Trickster speaks freshly where language has been blocked, gone dead, or lost its charm. Here again, Plato's intuition—that deceit and inventive speech are linked—holds, for usually language goes dead because cultural practice has hedged it in, and some shameless double-dealer is needed to get outside the rules and set tongues wagging again. (p. 76)

King became just such a shameless "double-dealer" by combining his gifts as a spiritual orator, political activist, and cultural hero into nonviolent confrontations that stirred up all sides of the cultural split, thus "setting tongues wagging again." On one side of the paradigm King opened a new space for national dialogue on the cultural problem of racism, and on the other, chaos amidst the old order. The result was a painful wielding of the truth long denied. And while the truth created a dialogue, it also collided with a national aggression living just under the surface of both sides of the racial wound. In the end, the work of the trickster marchers aimed at resolving the disjunction between the haves and have-nots in America. The archetypal trickster became the central force of the civil rights movement carried by the marchers and, implemented and tended to by King's extraordinary oracular gifts, wholly influencing the American spirit.

Keith Miller (1992), in his book *Voice of Deliverance*, states that King's gifts as a cultural unifier lay in his national appeal. Miller asserts,

> By incorporating into virtually all of his mainline sermons the old-fashioned, yet radical black demand for equality, King accomplished a feat that no one else had ever achieved. He reached white audiences and thereby turned the traditional black demand into something it had never been before—a mainstream American idea. (p. 85)

Indeed, King was advanced by the collective to participate in the role of the shaman trickster, or cultural healer and hero, because he could stand on either side of the divide and deliver on one side or the other a missing piece of the paradigm necessary for healing the racist split. Miller observes,

> Articulating the devilish paradox of good and evil also served the cause of civil rights. By embracing the paradox, King avoided ideologically equating his movement with pure goodness and his opponents with evil incarnate—an equation that Malcolm X and other radical leaders did not hesitate to make. King's decision had important consequences. Some reformers … call for justice to roll down like waters but are unwilling to build any irrigation ditches. By contrast, King not only called for justice to roll down like waters, he actually sat down with business leaders and government officials to channel and direct the waters of justice. His

argument about good and evil within each person granted him the flexibility to negotiate with allies and bargain with adversaries. (p. 84)

The trickster King became the master boundary crosser, and through his efforts to unify the country, called into being an otherwise unformed image of American democracy. Truly, the beauty of the trickster myth is that the trickster lays bare the moral dilemma, hence providing an opportunity for dialogue. King's healing powers of nonviolent philosophy could penetrate the raw affective emotion otherwise untouchable by many political and spiritual leaders. King understood implicitly that "a spiritual based nonviolence, one that truly seeks change from within has to engage deeply the spirits on both sides of a conflict" (Wink, 2000, p. 150). The civil rights movement exposed racism's ethical gap and, through nonviolent demonstrations, changed the national dialogue. Moreover, the gap demanded the moral bridge that Selma momentarily provided.

Though King's mercurial role could unify, it was not performed without tremendous personal sacrifice. He suffered immensely as a leader and was tortured from all sides of the movement. Jealousy and envy within the ranks of his organization (Southern Christian Leadership Conference (SCLC)) as well as other organizations such as the NAACP and SNCC threatened to dismantle the cause, as he continually managed the tension of opposing forces threatening to bring down the movement. Although among the vast majority of demonstrators and the African American community at large, King was "dubbed the black man's 'savior—America's Gandhi'" (McWhorter, 2001, p. 3), in various parts of the white community and the Federal Bureau of Investigation, King was seen as both a troublemaker and negative trickster who worked for communist-backed causes against American ideals and values (Garrow, 1981, p. 122). Indeed, King was a workaholic whose energy and reputation as a tireless leader preceded him. At the height of his career, he gave an astounding 200–300 public addresses per year, while constantly fighting depression and exhaustion (Miller, 1992, p. 67). Miller (1992) reports that King's "schedule never flagged—despite assassination attempts, death threats, jail sentences, and the weight of making life-and-death decisions while scrutinized by the entire world" (p. 67). Moreover, King's commitment to nonviolence gave him the capacity to suffer without reprisal in the face of severe persecution.

King's capacity to contain the sufferings of his people while holding a healing vision for the future endowed him with the mantle of a healer. His spiritual capacities thus aligned him with the trickster as shaman. According to Jung (1968), the spiritualism of the shaman embraces not only trickery, but also the wounded savior as the agent of healing. When describing Mercurius, he states,

His universality is co-extensive, so to speak, with that of shamanism, to which, as we know, the whole phenomenology of spiritualism belongs. There is something of the trickster in the character of the shaman and medicine-man, for he, too, often plays malicious jokes on people, only to fall victim in his turn to the vengeance of those whom he has injured … His approximation to the savior is an obvious consequence of this, in confirmation of the mythological truth that the "wounded wounder" is the agent of healing, and that the sufferer takes away suffering. (para. 457)

King embraced many roles of the archetypal trickster, such as suffering savior and shaman-healer, but his foremost role was that of the "wounded wounder," which gave him the capacity to bridge, suffer through, and unite the cultural divide, perhaps a wound within himself and the transgenerational wound of slavery. The irony of King's nonviolent acumen consisted of laying a new road of equality brick by brick while simultaneously blowing up the landscape of racial bias within the greater South, his hermetic ways inducing affective collective storms of aggression and love experienced by many as "mighty waters rolling down" from both heaven and hell.

The tactics King implemented with the demonstrators to bring consciousness to the South were familiar to the marchers, for, according to Malcolm Gladwell, King borrowed his strategy from the slave myths of Uncle Remus and its central characters, Brer Rabbit and Brer Fox (Harris, 1995). Malcolm Gladwell, in his book *David and Goliath* (2014), discussed the role of the trickster in African American mythology and its powerful effects on the civil rights demonstrators when utilized to gain equal rights. The civil rights tricksters changed history through employing tactics familiar to their ancestral slaves, whose victimized position in their relationship with the master forced them to be creative with their resources as a means of channeling their aggressions and manipulating their oppressors. These tactics were passed along generationally through myth and song.

According to Riggins Earl, Jr. in his book, *Dark Symbols, Obscure Signs* (2003), humor and suffering weaved within myth and song allowed mostly uneducated slaves the capacity to mediate suffering with each other as well as the means to record, preserve, and protect their heritage. Because slaves were subjected to anti-literacy laws in the Southern states, myth and song provided a safe format from which they could communicate with each other through codes embedded in a unique language which their white masters did not understand (pp. 72–73). These capacities to overcome suffering through subtle and obvious forms of manipulation and trickery unwittingly provided an outlet to freedom for the civil rights marchers in 1965 when the trickster tactics became the central psychological tool of the movement. Indeed, tactical tricks became common practice in nonviolent activism because they had a cumulative effect on the temperament of law enforcement officials. Trickster pranks wore the police officers down and eventually drove them to act out aggressively towards the demonstrators. For example, mass arrests in Selma became one way that law enforcement dealt with the demonstrators' disruption of peace, but even during the mass jailing, the marchers continued to aggravate the authorities. Charles Fager (1974), in his book *Selma 1965*, states,

> It took hours for all the demonstrators to be booked and taken upstairs to the county jail, which was the only facility large enough to hold them. Before long the people waiting to be processed began playing little tricks that drove the city policemen on duty up to the wall: lining up obstinately at the white water fountain, switching the 'white for colored' signs on the bathrooms, and generally acting considerably less than intimated. (p. 51)

With the help of one of his key lieutenants, Wyatt Walker, King utilized tried and true slave tactics to trick law enforcement officials like Clark in Selma, into "tipping his hand" (Gladwell, 2013, p. 181), or revealing the white man's shadow side and entrapping him in his own destructive tendencies. One such tactic was illusion. In Birmingham, Walker captured the attention of the press by tricking them into thinking that hundreds of people were marching into the courthouse, when, in fact, only a few comprised a loop through front and back doors and around the block. Walker would later confess that to build a new morality to "get the job done," his sleight-o-hand tactics would be considered morally questionable at best. Walker recalls,

> At times I would accommodate or alter my morality for the sake of getting a job done because I was the guy having to deal with the results.... . I did it consciously; I had no choice. I wasn't dealing with a moral situation when I dealt with a Bull Connor. (as cited in Gladwell, 2013, p. 176, Kindle version)

Gladwell reported,

> Walker loved to play tricks on Connor. "I have come to Birmingham to ride the Bull," he announced, eyes twinkling, upon his arrival. He might put on a Southern drawl and call in some imaginary complaint to the local police about "niggers" headed somewhere in a protest, sending them off on a wild goose chase. "Oh, man, it was a great time to be alive," he said, recalling the antics he got up to in Birmingham. (pp. 176–177)

Walker's behaviors reflect Hermes's stealthy ways. Like Hermes, who steals cattle from Apollo to highlight cultural misappropriation, Walker may have had to do something morally questionable (a sleight of hand) in order to capture the attention of the aggressor. He and King understood that direct confrontation could be extraordinarily dangerous in such incendiary circumstances, and they were willing to break certain rules in order to accomplish the job. According to Gladwell (2013), in the Birmingham campaign,

King and Walker were under no illusions that they could fight racism the conventional way. They could not defeat Bull Connor at the polls, or in the streets, or in the court of law. They could not match him strength for strength. What they could do, though, was play Brer Rabbit and try to get Connor to throw them in the briar patch. (p. 17)

The briar patch Gladwell refers to comes from the *The Tar Baby.* (also known as *Tar Baby*). The origins of *The Tar Baby* are speculative and extend from India to Japan, the Philippines, Europe, the Americas, and Africa. According to Aurelio Espinoza, a literary scholar and expert on *The Tar Baby*, 267 versions of the story extend across the globe, with various scholars claiming different countries of origin other than Africa. Although the tale has been identified primarily with Africa and was brought to America via the slaves, many other countries claim ancestral and cultural roots to the tale (Wagner, 2017, pp. 4–12).

In the thread of the story, Brer Fox, Brer Rabbit's nemesis, attempts to trap Brer Rabbit and murder him, as he is sick of the rabbit's bossiness and trickery. In the story as retold by Joel Chandler Harris (1995), Brer Fox designs a tar-shaped baby that he props up in the middle of the road, hoping that the wandering Brer Rabbit will entrap himself in the sticky mess, thereby allowing Brer Fox to kill him. Brer Fox hides in the bushes waiting for the caper to unfold, as it certainly does. Brer Rabbit becomes infuriated at the tar baby when it does not respond to his nicety: "Good morning, stranger! Is it hot enough for you?" (p. 45). The longer Brer Rabbit is met with silence, the angrier he becomes until he loses his temper, unleashing his frustrations on the inanimate, sticky figure, quickly becoming mired in tar himself. The fox, observing from the bushes, gleefully giggles at the success of his diabolical plotting.

Emerging from the bushes, Brer Fox begins to negotiate all the ways that Brer Rabbit will meet his demise: roast him, hang him, or drown him. Brer Rabbit, the master trickster, pleads, "Drown me if you must, sink me as deep as you want, Brer Fox, but please, PLEASE don't throw me into the briar patch!" (Harris, 1995, p. 53). Brer Fox taunts Brer Rabbit with all ways he could kill him, and finally, he decides to throw Brer Rabbit into the briar patch. Waiting to hear the gurgles and whimpers of pain and final death, Brer Fox is dismayed that his anticipation is met with silence until he hears Brer Rabbit calling his name. He turns to find Brer Rabbit combing the tar out of his fur with a wood chip. Says Brer Rabbit: "I told you not to throw me in there. Maybe next time you'll listen" (Harris, 1995, p. 54).

Brer Rabbit is a survivor whose trickster ways keep him one step ahead of annihilation and illustrate his capacity to survive in conditions defined by the predator Brer Fox, who desires to taunt, bully, and plot murder on poor Brer Rabbit, whose life consists of a certain hellish existence. Indeed, as a tale of survival, the Brer Rabbit stories became a salve to slaves whose daily lives consisted of seemingly infinite servitude. Although the tale is informative in terms of Rabbit's capacity to survive under oppressive circumstances, it is even more enriching for what is reveals psychologically—what we do with our aggression in the face of being victimized by violence. The tale points to a timeless universal, spiritual question; "how do we transform our anger non-violently?" Jim Douglass in the book *Peace is the Way Writings of Non-violence from the Fellowship of Reconciliation* (2000) asserts, "A simple truth at the root of nonviolence is that we can't change an evil or injustice from the outside" (Wink, 2000, p. 149). As Earl (2003) so aptly states, "the rabbit symbol was designed to prevent slaves from dealing honestly with their own legitimate feelings of raging anger, which they were required to repress daily" (p. 146). Slaves had to learn to be passive as a means of survival, and mythological tales like Brer Rabbit and Fox enabled them to cope with their rage at being oppressed. However, these tales would be used to their ancestors' advantage in the civil rights movement, where they could openly begin transforming their aggression through nonviolent means.

In racist enactments a particular tactical ancestral pacifism enabled the marchers to hold the tension against violence without acting violently, thus forcing the white man to "tip his hand," thus, entrapping the white man in the tar baby. As such, Brer Rabbit and Brer Fox mythology lays bare the unattended, unexplored unconscious dynamics of racism. The marchers in Selma set a trap for Clark and got him to act out his racist aggressions while they were then able to capitalize on such aggression by using the media as the lens of consciousness to the nation.

Through the viaduct of the collective unconscious and the transgenerational trauma of slavery, the *The Tar Baby* tale unconsciously informed King and the marchers of a new way to use trickster tactics to reveal the shadow of the other. The trickster archetype encompasses a prism of psychic images, all unconscious, defined by affect, all holding the capacity for confusion, illusion, psychic transformation, stagnation, and insanity, all characterized by a myriad of internal and external conditions united in a dynamic manifestation that throws one's world order into chaos while opening up the possibility for a new order. Such was the goal and focus of Kingian trickster tactics. Such trickery can be seen in Fox's capacity to bring Rabbit to a full froth of rage entrapping him in his own sticky aggression (his shadow). Rabbit projectively identifies with Fox, enacting Fox's aggression, thus trapping himself in his own anger. In order to free himself from Fox and his pending death, he knows no other way but to trick the trickster. Once free, Fox is left holding the bag of his anger and thirst for revenge while the Rabbit runs free. The lack of consciousness sets the paradigm up to begin again. Poor Brer Rabbit does not see that he becomes the very thing he hates when he unconsciously identifies with the aggressor, Brer Fox, who harms him. As in the complex of racism, the voicelessness of the tar baby exacerbates the violent cycle between the two characters, which might otherwise be dialogically mediated through by a healthy observing ego.

The archetypal trickster is a psychic pattern or psychic image which Fox and Rabbit enact an, in which the two characters replicate intra-psychic split forces interacting in a pattern of gotcha. This hide and go seek represents ways in which we may collude with or avoid a truth inside of ourselves when trapped in our shadow, unable to recognize our destructive tendencies, thus avoiding an inner responsibility. The pattern also represents the ways in which we may get others to act out an aggression which we refuse to face within ourselves. Fox and Rabbit replicate the insanity of remaining stuck in an unconscious world split off from the potential of self-awareness. An observing ego may untangle the quagmire- and insanity-making trickster pattern. Like the sheriff who gets more enraged at the demonstrator's refusal to acknowledge his demands, Brer Rabbit and Brer Fox become caught over and over again in their mutual sadomasochistic pattern. Left unchecked, they become dependent on each other's call and response as well as the repetition of emotional abuse which each inflicts upon the other. One can imagine that with each dramatic enactment of escaping the trap, the aggression only grows stronger in each party, thus engendering quick-wittedness in their desire to outsmart and entrap the other. Their mutual dependency of violence shapes the masochism that chains them together, while setting up an internal condition of a calcified, malignant learned helplessness which entombs them both in a victimized position defined by a projection on the other as the problem from which they can never escape.

Brer Rabbit and Fox cannot change until they know internally what ails them and how they collude in their own suffering. In this mutually sustained relationship, within the individual lies the hunter, the hunted, and the trapped. However, if Rabbit could become aware of his shadow; his dependency on Brer Fox, he wouldn't need to trick the Fox into freeing him. If the Fox could recognize his need of the Rabbit, his vengeful feelings might diminish. Through a recognition of mutual dependency, the rightful side of dominance and submission could emerge, the two characters shifting between the two positions in a power paradigm of relatedness, the birth of psychic consciousness. Instead, there is chaos. Trickster is the initiator of turmoil, a turmoil that may lead to change or which may not, depending on which way consciousness tips.

Historically, tricksters enter the fray in a culture ripe for change and begin the process of systematic dismantling social patterns through their tricks and deceptions (Hyde, 1998, p. 205).

Ostensibly, the trickster has the uncanny capacity to locate the central thread of a cultural complex and tug at the defining core issue, laying bare its ugly truth, which then destabilizes the system's undergirding, leaving it ripe for reconstruction. The question becomes whether the culture is prepared for the ugly truth and whether it can withstand the deconstruction required for the change.

The civil rights movement of the 1950s and 60s proposed such deconstruction-construction cycle, led by the marchers whose tactics disoriented those in oppositional forces, resulting in the prey becoming the predator, and the predator the prey. Indeed, "in evolutionary theory, the tension between predator and prey is one of the great engines that has driven the creation of intelligence itself, each side successively and ceaselessly responding to each other" (Hyde, 1998, p. 20). Trickster energy affects and perhaps *is* the experience of perception itself, which informs intelligence. When perception is forming or transforming, one wonders what is happening. Time slips the knot of a linear experience as this energy releases something from the storehouse of the collective unconscious.

The shadow side of any activist campaign is that it serves a cultural faction seeking justice for their own self-empowerment. Political movements can fail, and often do, because the intentions of the activists are not driven by an organic spiritual indwelling arising from the collective unconscious but from an urge to power, a false self, formed from a position of victimhood within a marginalized segment of society. According to Douglass,

> in any attitude of resistance to the state there is kind of demonic underside, power turned upside down, which wishes to gain the upper hand. Civil disobedience which is not done as prayer is especially vulnerable to the other side. (Wink, 2000, p. 149)

Campaigns for justice that arise as attempts to oppress rather than free both sides of the illusion of power become caught, like Brer Rabbit and Brer Fox, in an eternal struggle for power, a jack-in-the-box game of gotcha.

Hermes has a lot to say about how consciousness can be raised in a relationship trapped in an emotionally stagnant state. Sometimes, the construct has to be completely dismantled, as in a bad marriage. Sometimes, what appears to be the truth is a falsity that created the oppressive situation to begin with and must be transformed through Hermes' trickery, again. His ordering of the universe cannot be distinguished, predicted, or controlled; it occurs on his own time and terms. Sometimes, healing lies in a particular nonviolent state of waiting.

References

Brown, N. O. (1947). *Hermes the Thief: the Evolution of a Myth.* Madison: University of Wisconsin Press.

DeVinney, C. C. (Director). (1987). *Eyes on the Prize, Part 6: The Bridge to Freedom* [Motion Picture].

Earl, Jr. Riggins R., (2003). *Dark Symbols, Obscure Signs: God, Self, and Community in the Slave Mind.* New York: Maryknoll.

Fager, C. (1974). *Selma 1965: The March that Changed the South.* New York: Charles Schribner's and Sons.

Garrow, D. (1981). *The FBI and Martin Luther King, Jr.* New York, London: W.W. Norton and Company.

Gladwell, M. (2013). *David and Goliath.* New York, Boston, London: Little, Brown and Company.

Harris, J. C. (1995). *The Classic Tales of Brer Rabbit.* Philadelphia, London: Running Press.

Hyde, L. (1998). *Trickster Makes This World: Mischief, Myth and Art.* New York: Farrar, Straus and Giroux.

Jung, C. (1968). *The Archetypes of the Collective Unconscious. The Collected Works of C.G. Jung Vol. 9.i.* Princeton: Princeton University Press.

McWhorter, D. (2001). *Carry Me Home: Birmingham, Alabama: The Climactic Battle of the Civil Rights Revolution.* New York: Simon & Schuster.

Miller, K. D. (1992). *Voice of Deliverance.* New York: Free Press.

Wagner, B. (2017). *The Tar Baby: A Global History.* Princeton: Princeton University Press.

Wink, W. (2000). *Peace is the Way: Writings on Nonviolence from the Fellowship of Reconciliation.* Maryknoll: Orbis Books.

Chapter 7

Analytic interpretation of the march

Irony was the word for the day. It was Friday, August 6, 1965, in Washington, DC, as the leaders of the civil and political establishments gathered in the White House to sign the Voting Rights Act. Among the nation's leaders stood Reverend Martin Luther King, Jr., Reverend Ralph Abernathy, Rosa Parks, and John Lewis. President Lyndon Johnson, seated at his desk with King standing to his left, signed the Act into law, handing King one of the many pens used in the calligraphy that constituted the letters in Johnson's name (https://www.nbclearn.com).

The relationship between King and Johnson had become especially solidified on Monday, March 15, 1965, when Johnson gave his famous speech, "We Shall Overcome." The speech, designed to unite the country behind the movement in Selma and bring voting rights home to African Americans, went beyond momentarily uniting the country. It also fulfilled the destiny of many activists who had been carrying the nation's vision for a new moral order.

In Montgomery, Lewis, King, and others had watched Johnson deliver his infamous speech. Lewis reported that King was so deeply moved that he could be seen wiping tears from his eyes (Kotz, 2005, p. 312). After the speech, King phoned Johnson, acknowledging the historical moment. "It is ironic, Mr. President, that after a century, a southern white President would help lead the way toward the salvation of the negro" (Kotz, p. 314).

The Johnson–King relationship had been a formal dance comprised of two great personalities vying for positions of power within their own worlds and between each other. Johnson found in King an ally whose acumen for strategic political maneuverings equaled his own. King understood Johnson and his desire to make a difference in the lives of African Americans, yet he also knew that behind Johnson's actions lay political and self-motivated intentions. Indeed, Johnson had power, and he masterfully wielded it, sometimes at the cost of his conscience, such as in America's involvement in the Vietnam war, the breaking point of the King–Johnson relationship.

The work that King and his ministerial counterparts cultivated and delivered from prior generations informed the archetypal image of democracy which emerged through the civil rights movement. Indeed, the collective located in King the human source for the alchemical transformation to come in 1955, when civil rights activist Rosa Parks refused to give up her seat on a bus. This event brought King, Parks' minister, into the fold, where he would step up to lead the bus boycotts. For the next thirteen years, King would lead the civil rights movement.

King spearheaded the civil rights campaigns in Montgomery, Albany, Birmingham, and Selma, Alabama, as well as Washington, DC. He had a direct impact on the passing of the 1964 and 1965 civil rights acts through his negotiations with President Lyndon Johnson. The achievement of voting rights for Blacks became an exceedingly important piece of legislation, for it was designed to bring into alignment what the nation's conscience lacked; the promise of freedom, liberty, and justice for all races. It was the civil rights movement that, once again, made America conscious of the constitutional hypocrisy contained in racism.

The American narrative and the archetypal experience of democracy revolves around the existential experience of freedom socially constructed and legally negotiated through the vote. The vote is a sacred act that unites the one to the many in a dream for the country and its future. Freedom itself is a metaphysical quest, a form of activism that engages the internal and external worlds (Combs, 2014, p. 5). Without the vote, the individual lives on an island alone, cut off from others and the possibility of creatively participating in the process of collective development. Selma is the story of America's moral sickness of racism and its collective attempts at wellness through the integration of shadow via nonviolent interventions.

The civil rights movement wasn't the nation's first attempt at psychological wholeness. The constitution has been ratified many times to enforce, define, and clarify the right to vote, with each ratification representing a nodal point of consciousness in the nation's psychological development: the passing of the 15th Amendment in 1870, granting the Black male vote; the passing of the 19th Amendment in 1919, giving women, including African American women, the right to vote; and finally, the 1965 passage of the Voting Rights Act. Despite these constitutional amendments, voting rights are still being manipulated by political parties and local governing authorities targeting specific voters (Timm, 2019).

In psychological development, the instinctive development of the individual personality is guided by the process of individuation, the ego's attempt at wholeness through its relationship with the outer world. The bidirectional flow between one's inner and outer worlds is critical to the unfolding of the personality. This process is instinctive, active, and dynamic. Its central dynamism revolves around the mediation of instinctual violent psychic forces with love and consciousness. Love and consciousness can only be truly achieved through relatedness with the other; thus, humans are essentially relationship-seeking beings. The active, dynamic aspects of personality unfold through the process of relationship building. Nonviolent activism is a cultivator of life against the forces of violence that threaten desired connection. Jung's concept of individuation can therefore be directly linked to nonviolent activism and its bidirectional effect on the individual and culture. Jungian scholar Andrew Samuels (1993/2001) discussed the intersection of psyche, politics, and social activism at length. Nonviolent theory is a springboard into Samuel's field of thinking in terms of collective development. Nonviolent theory plays an equally important role in the development of cultural consciousness in that the intervention of nonviolence has a powerful effect on the integrity of complexes.

Collective nonviolent activism is based on a set of principles, part philosophical, part strategic, designed to cripple political and social systems that are defined by authoritarian violence (Montiel and Christie, 2008; Kurlansky, 2006). Christie and Montiel (2008) contend that nonviolent change in culture does not occur without an interpersonal, singular shift of the same kind within the individuals involved in the execution of a nonviolent movement. They explained,

> The concept of transition connects the smaller analytical layers of human agency with macro contextual conditions. Individuals bring to each transition their histories of human experiences and dispositions, select themselves into a transition process, and are influenced by the social change ... We posit a parallel yet distinct phenomenon occurring at the collective level. (p. 266)

The authors noted that nonviolence thus involves the bidirectional participation of micro and macro systems. The protest in Selma demonstrated the individuation process in action through the "bidirectional participation of micro and macros systems," or connection between the individual and cultural complexes explicitly as they related to the archetypal world of the collective unconscious. Thomas Singer and Catherine Kaplinsky (2010), who wrote about cultural complexes in analysis, stated,

> Cultural complexes are based on frequently repeated historical experiences that have taken root in the collective psyche of a group and in the psyches of the individual members of a group. And they express archetypal values of the group. As such, cultural complexes can be thought of as the fundamental building blocks of an inner sociology. (p. 8)

They explained that cultural complexes are formed within the cultural unconscious of a group of people and specified that "one can conceptualize the cultural unconscious as closer to the surface of ego-consciousness than the collective unconscious, from which we understand the archetypal patterns to originate" (pp. 1–2). Separating the cultural complex from the collective unconscious, they said, gives "more careful consideration to the uniqueness of different cultures, including their separate cultural complexes" (p. 6). Psychic elements within the cultural unconscious can combine to create the perfect storm, releasing within the individual and the cultural complex enormous psychic shifts, which can explain the etiology of cultural zeitgeists and their effects on the individual.

In the case of Selma, the identified group of carriers of the cultural unconscious were those living in Selma as well as those Blacks in the civil rights movement who came to Selma in protest. The marchers and the officials themselves were carriers of the racist complex and were also part of the historical collective trauma of racism, a complex which, at its core, was defined by the archetype of master–slave; however, the marchers also carried an emerging national consciousness, which challenged the complex's breadth and depth. The Blacks defined one half of the split within the complex: the oppressed other, whose identities were shaped by their individual experiences of racism as well as the transgenerational wound of slavery.

Those in Selma who intended to preserve the status quo were also carriers of the complex. They formed the other half of the split defined by power, dominance, and violence. They too carried the transgenerational wound of racism. Whites who supported segregation and Black racial bias consisted of some upper-class Whites but, mainly, angry lower-income Whites, who aimed to keep what little they had (Fager, 1974, p. 8). Both sides were defensively armed with economic, psychological, and emotional reasons for their positions, defined by slavery, the Civil War, and reconstruction. Within the complex, both sides carried the problem as well as the solution to racism, should it become accessible through the alchemical procedure of shadow integration.

In the South, the embers of racism were primarily stoked by lower-class Whites who hated people of color. These racists were threatened by the economic potential of Blacks and were angry about the upper-class Whites who scooped up most of the economic prosperity. These economic conditions set the stage for Blacks to be the perfect projective container for the fear and hatred these lower-class Whites could not face within themselves (Fager, 1974, p. 8). Giving rights to Blacks was certain to explode an already combustible situation.

From January to March 1965, the demonstrators marched regularly from Selma's Brown Chapel African Methodist Episcopal Church to the Dallas County Courthouse demanding to register for the vote. Each march was initiated from the nonviolent temenos created in Brown's Chapel. There, King and his lieutenants would meet with the congregation and discuss the nonviolent tactics and strategies to be utilized in the day's events, which would be followed by de-briefings.

In Selma, King chose his adversary carefully. He needed someone who would step into the role of the abusive other so that he could enlist his marchers in an enactment of the racial trauma and capture the conscience of the nation through the eye of the camera. King found his match in Sheriff Jim

Clark. Clark was just the kind of person the movement needed to demonstrate racism as the marchers had experienced it for so long. King homed in on Clark and planned to capitalize on his combativeness (Garrow, 1978, p. 159). Consciousness weakens a constellated complex, and in Selma, Clark became an important shadow element that exposed the core of the racial complex. Sheriff Clark's persona enabled him to disguise his racism with the authority that law enforcement gave him as keeper of the peace; however, Clark's aggressiveness also made him a highly charged shadow element, because he carried not just his individual complexes but also the "archetypal values of the group" within the cultural complex (Singer and Kaplinsky, 2010, p. 8). Clark justified his racist attitude and violent tendencies by labeling the marchers "outside agitators" who were disturbing the peace and breaking the law.

For the demonstrators, each march served as a nonviolent bid for dominance in the face of Clark's aggression. Utilizing nonviolent tactics such as verbal confrontation, singing, sitting silently, and praying, the marchers confronted Clark at the courthouse. In response, Clark's combustible temper would bring him to full froth. The media, intentionally drawn into the honey trap, would record the violent enactment(s), thus reflecting to the general public the immorality of racism. The protestors were trained to resist violent retaliation, for in retaliation, they risk becoming that which they hated: the violent other. The news media became the discerning psychic mechanism of developing consciousness, a mirror to the nation's split off shadow. Consequently, with each enactment, the White person's eyes were opened, if ever so briefly, to the image of violence and racism living within.

Intra-psychically, the camera represents the process of introjection, the psychological, emotional, and somatic ingestion of life's experiences. Once introjected, the information is then processed as perspective, shaped through the psycho-historical filters of identity: family, culture, and race. Psycho-historical filters become the material of projection unless self-reflection or consciousness intervenes. With the assistance of the media, King hoped that nonviolence would break the cycle of racist projection that shaped the complex. Ultimately, the persistent enactments of the cultural trauma of racism, titrated by nonviolent activism, had a kaleidoscopic effect upon the collective. Over the course of weeks and months, the consistent implementation of nonviolence was key for inducing reflection within the collective.

For those individuals who could reflect on their participation in the projection of racism, the suffering of truth became the psychic nutrient for infusing the feminine into the complex. The news media's images of the enactments gave voice to the marginalized, who had long been brutalized into an oppressive silence. Many Whites were awakened from their projections and joined the marginalized in search of a new ethic. These people all carried the seeds of a new cultural consciousness, for they carried the shadow elements of the complex long denied by the majority—contents which the old ethic lacked, and the new ethic demanded (Neumann, 1990, pp. 30–33). The bridge to a new ethic required a consciousness born of suffering. Self-reflective suffering opens the door to something higher than an ego-oriented experience: agape, the connection to the greater good through divine love.

As the news media vigilantly recorded the demonstrations, the marchers assiduously worked to dissolve the defenses within the town's law enforcement officials through nonviolent love. During one particular demonstration, marchers were holding a prayer vigil when outside observers witnessed "a trooper moved to tears by their appeals, and another visibly praying with them (the demonstrators)" (Fager, 1974, p. 126). Whatever unknown reasons existed for the officer's expression of feeling, it demonstrated to witnesses that something was consciously shifting. It was not uncommon for the trickster marchers to affect enforcement officials in a myriad of ways. Although the marchers' antics commonly stirred up their oppressors' aggression, they also induced empathy, momentarily releasing both sides of the split from the complex that had defined them for centuries.

According to Neumann (1969/1990), when one can face the shadow mirrored by the other, this makes one not only individually more capable of managing one's own contradictions and less projective but also makes one "an agent for immunization of the collective" (p. 130). He explained, "Moreover, an individual's shadow is invariably bound up with the collective shadow of his group, and as he digests his own evil, a fragment of the collective evil is invariably co-digested at the same time" (p. 130). The one's interrelatedness with one's own shadow thus depotentiates the cultural complex and "leads to an inner liberation of the collective, which in part at least is redeemed from this evil" (p. 130).

On the shadow side of the complex, aggression and violence can increase when the aggressor's projections cannot be dissolved due to deeply entrenched psychological defenses. Sheriff Clark's aggression towards the marchers, for example, only escalated as time wore on. The movement was beginning to wear him down, his prickly temperament cracking under the pressure. Clark's aggression eventually landed him in the hospital with chest pains, at one point defensively stating to a reporter: "The niggers are givin' me a heart attack" (as cited in Fager, 1974, p. 68). Clark may have rather died than convert, yet the other officers' tears indicated that something deeper was happening: perhaps guilt and remorse were seeping in, grief was bubbling up through their defenses. Indeed, these two factions of law enforcement represented the spectrum of possible affective change within the complex. Some individuals taking on a new perspective, whereas others, like Clark, exhibited little capacity for consciousness, their aggression becoming stuck in the body, inducing physical suffering.

Physical suffering was experienced by the marchers who could not metabolize their own aggression into consciousness. Many had to be prescribed sedatives to calm their nerves, rattled from the ongoing exposure to violence

(Ghaemi, 2011, p. 111). Tactical nonviolence poses hazards when its practitioners are unable or incapable of integrating their own shadows. One's inability to resist violence keeps the transcendent function stuck in the body.

In her article, "When Meaning Gets Lost in the Body: Psychosomatic Disturbances as a Failure of the Transcendent Function," Jungian analyst Mara Sidoli (1993) surmised that early traumatic experiences too painful to assimilate become caught in the body when deeply painful material threatens to break through to consciousness. More specifically, she stated, "The upsurge of affect reaches the threshold of the 'zone of meaning,' appearing to short-circuit it and to discharge itself into the body or into bodily organs. Thus, the body provides the last bulwark against integration" (p. 1).

In Clark's case, he may have suffered an early trauma greater than what his ego could hold, consequently causing a psychological split. His only means of coping may have been to suppress the rage, lock it away deep in his unconscious. In order to heal, one must be able to feel that trauma, titrating the experience with nonviolent love. If the truth of the wound is ignored, it may become an inner psychic entity, or voice, which taunts the ego, demanding justice for the hurt. This inner voice manifests as the master–slave dynamic, of which the ego is unconscious, but which rules the inner house. In order to survive the violence, the ego identifies with the aggressor (Ferenczi, 1933), or archetypal inner master, and begins acting the inner tyranny out in the outer world, making the other the slave through violence and aggression. The loneliness and isolation experienced by the ego in this sadistic paradigm creates an inner slave, the victimized other within the split, which becomes dependent on the sadist for recognition by the ego.

The goal of healing would be to make the inner master–slave dynamic conscious to the ego. The individual would have to suffer through the trauma again, but through grief, self-reflection, humility, and love, learn how to forgive the person(s) whom they perceive to be their captor. Then the inner master would find no urgency or purpose is punishing those who live in the outer world, for the roots of the loving master would diminish the purpose of the negative master. This inner–outer pattern, when mediated by nonviolence, changes the paradigm when consciousness is born.

With King's guidance, the nonviolent demonstrations penetrated the American soul, impaling its inflated ego with shadow contents (enactments), thus releasing from the collective unconscious a ratified image of psychological wholeness through the symbol of the vote. Like Gandhi, King was the great individual who bridged the divide. His hermetic capacities allowed for what would be considered riotous resistance to become the pursuit of a new moral order. The individual is constantly challenged in the quest against current collective values, requiring the "Great Individual" (Neumann, 1969/1990, p. 61) to free the collective from its moral blindness. As hero to the movement, the "Great Individual" travels into the unconscious to retrieve the pearl of consciousness from the depths and deliver it to the masses. According to Neumann,

> In the primal stage [of group consciousness], when the individual
> members of the group are still to a large extent undifferentiated, the
> 'Great Individual' will represent the 'mana- personality'; he will be, in
> a sense, the Self of the group, its creative centre, and it will be from
> him in his capacity as leader and creator that the collective will
> receive its values ... The Great Individual acts as a founder and
> initiator in every sphere—that is to say he is a spiritual progenitor. He
> performs this function as a ... founder of an ethic. Ethical values are
> created as a result of a revelation by the 'Voice' to the Founder
> Individual. (pp. 61–62)

As the spiritual progenitor of the civil rights movement, King became the
sacrificial lamb offered for the development of the collective's new moral
order and would give birth to the archetype of nonviolent activism in
America. His mana was especially threatening because his power swayed his
followers, many of whom relied on his philosophical nonviolent capacity to
guide them in what their consciousness lacked. King thus became the image
of America's shadow in racism: the empowered, self-possessed, conscious
slave to the unconscious, hubris-filled, master.

To be genuinely free, the Whites and the Blacks need access to their inner
opposite other. The slave needs access to an inner empowering, loving master,
whereas the master needs access to an inner dependent, vulnerable, loving
slave, which will cure the master of hubris. If each can see the other as the
cure for their ills, the rightful, interdependent relationship can emerge. The
interdependent, whole relationship can emerge when each refuses violence
while concomitantly seeking common ground in the connection. The key to
refusing violence or nonviolence is to *fully feel* aggression in the face of a
threat while subsequently reflecting on how the other lives within. This is the
essence of nonviolent consciousness.

The outcome of each march demonstrated a micromovement in consciousness as the ego confronted shadow. Those who could carry consciousness
became deeply affected by the broadcasting of the racial enactments and
began seeking connection through local activism of their own, thus contributing to the emerging moral order; however, the shadow side of the
movement catalyzed unconscious archetypal defenses that were resistant to
nonviolent action. These defenses would shape the violent riots that were to
come after Selma.

As the marches spread between January and March much of the country
moved into alignment with the marchers. A collective initiation was at hand
through the Self's revelation of the new moral order. With initiation comes
sacrifice, and unfortunately, the marchers could not foresee that the sacrifice
would come in three deaths, the first being that of Jimmie Lee Jackson, who
was shot while protesting in Marion, Alabama.

James Bevel, one of King's lieutenants, had a serendipitous experience while walking around outside of the Torch Motel in Marion, Alabama, an idea for the march to Montgomery (Fager, 1974, p. 81). Later that same day, Jackson would die from his injuries. Within eight days, the marchers would attempt their first crossing to Montgomery.

Bloody Sunday occurred with the first attempt to reach Montgomery. Approaching the Edmund Pettus Bridge, the demonstrators carried with them hundreds of years of ancestral slavery and trauma as well as a dream for redemption. It would be through nonviolent action and the holding of *ahimsa* that time and space would bridge the past and present in an attempt to heal the ancestral suffering on both sides of the split. But upon reaching the other side of the bridge, the demonstrators were gassed, beaten, and forced back to Brown's Chapel.

The demonstration represented the psychic developmental push within the nation as the two sides of the split made contact: one side needed to maintain the status quo through dominance and power, whereas the other side attempted to integrate shadow via nonviolent activism, the rightful assertion of power. The union or bridging of these two forces reflects the self's attempt at a relationship with the ego. The ego must be opened to the bid for rightful dominance by the self.

The collective cries of outrage over the unprovoked attack and enactment of the master–slave paradigm had a powerful effect on the nation's conscience, indicating that the collective complex had been affected, its integrity diminished through the infusion of nonviolence. Through the enactment of the master–slave, America experienced a glimpse of the country's hypocrisy in the founders intent of freedom for all Americans. The nonviolent action of the marchers practicing *satyagraha* and *ahimsa* along with Kingian nonviolence challenged the nation's patriarchate and its authoritarian superego, the nation's unconscious attitude towards authority (Singer and Kimbles, 2004, p. 160).

After Bloody Sunday, King called upon other religious leaders to join him on Tuesday, March 9, for the second attempt to reach Montgomery. Within two days, approximately1,500 people of all colors and creeds gathered for the march on Turnaround Tuesday.

With the death of Jimmie Lee Jackson and the violence of Bloody Sunday, King strongly considered canceling the march, due to his fear of more violence. He turned to President Johnson for support, but before negotiations could be completed, King would change his mind several times. King was caught in a double bind. To proceed on the bridge, he would be breaking a Johnson-mandated federal injunction forbidding him to march. In so doing, he would jeopardize his relationship with Johnson and, subsequently, the passing of the voting rights bill. To delay the process would throw the movement into chaos, causing deeper cracks in an already strained civil rights system (Kotz, 2005, pp. 292–294).

Johnson was politically entangled in a similar double bind. He knew he needed King on his side, but he felt that in supporting the marches, he could be perceived to be "stirring up the marches," and in not supporting the marches, he risked more violence (Kotz, 2005, pp. 289–291). Ultimately, the direction in which consciousness would fall was yet to be determined. Each man's trickster ways had to be surrendered to something greater. After much negotiation with Leroy Collins, the President's Community Relations Director, King decided he would try to turn his people around, but with no guarantee that they would follow. In the end, no one knew what he would do.

"In the end," to Ultimately, King steered the demonstrators toward the Edmund Pettus Bridge for a second attempt at crossing. Upon reaching the far side of the bridge, King knelt and prayed, rose, and hesitated, then turned around on the bridge, his people following. This action set a firestorm of anger in motion by those on his side; for example, "a livid James Forman denounced King's behavior as a 'classic example of trickery against the people'" (Garrow, 1978, p. 405). Indeed, it seemed that neither party could outsmart the other. Little did the marchers know that the surrender would bring the movement to its goal.

The aversion of death on the bridge brought Johnson and King into a coupling that would be even more solidified later that evening, when Reverend James Reeb, a White minister from Boston, was attacked and killed by White racists while on his way home from dinner. The death of Reeb linked President Johnson directly to King and a determination to end the violence. This alignment would transform the moment in the movement, as the nation's outpouring of rage had to be contained by Johnson, who understood the cultural implications of the historical moment.

In the *Book of Symbols* (Archive for Research in Archetypal Symbolism, 2010), the bridge is designated as a symbol of spiritual union: "Psyche appears to support the separation of consciousness from the unconscious, but also a bridging that brings them into creative relationship" (p. 626). By walking across the bridge and holding a meditative, prayerful vigil, King was neither breaking the law by marching nor cooperating with evil by not marching. He held the tension of not knowing what to do, and by that action, bridged what had been, until that moment in time, two splits in the culture. The African American won the support of the government, and law enforcement, choosing not to retaliate, won the support of the nation. The withholding of violence for the sake of a greater good unified the opposites, creating an unconscious opening for the emergence of the third, the symbol. The moment of silence on the bridge ushered in a new paradigm: a creative act engendered by the collective unconscious.

To proceed on the bridge in the same manner as on Bloody Sunday could have indeed led to more violence, yet the supplication by all parties on the bridge indicated that a shift in consciousness had occurred on both sides. Intra-psychically, the events on the bridge revealed that a peeling back of projections had occurred, indicating that the rightful master and slave lived within and without, the defenses had been penetrated, and a violent enactment had been averted. The officials did not subscribe to violence, and the marchers did not rely on their usual tactics of trickery to get the white man to tip his hand.

Turnaround Tuesday, however, had deeply compromised King's position as the hero in the movement. Indeed, he had committed trickery against his people, not against law enforcement officials. By defying a court order, he had potentially alienated himself from the government and had compromised any position he might have had as a negotiator. Moreover, by turning around on the bridge, King had created acrimonious feelings from within both the Student Nonviolent Coordinating Committee (SNCC) and the Southern Christian Leadership Conference (SCLC). Strung up by both sides of the movement, King's image of the hero faded, and his suffering for a collective idea changed into the image of the martyr.

Turnaround Tuesday ushered in a series of events that paved the way for the marchers to wind their way to Montgomery. The President's full support of the movement was evident in a series of national speeches advocating for the rights of the demonstrators and their wish to march to Montgomery. King and Johnson now sat on the side of a great dream for all men: the right to be counted as equally important in the eyes of the government and the chance that, through a vote of democracy, one man's voice might set the stage to change a nation.

Within a few weeks, the movement was granted access to Montgomery, and the legislation drawn up by Johnson as an amendment to the Civil Rights Act of 1964 was transformed into the Voting Rights Act, which meant that the marchers would be granted their wish to march to Montgomery.

On March 21, the marchers set off to the Edmund Pettus Bridge for the last time, with a pervading sense of justice. Voting rights legislation was finally making its way through the bureaucratic channels of government. Any doubts the marchers carried about the future were set aside that day so that they could fully experience justice on their side. As the marchers crested the bridge, they were greeted by the National Guard lining the roads and ushering them home to Montgomery.

The crossing represented the sudden movement in consciousness from an old order to the beginning of the new ethic. The few carriers of consciousness who began their journey at the inception of the civil rights movement in the 1940s had reached the crest of the Edmund Pettus Bridge along with multitudes beyond measure, people of all colors, also becoming carriers of consciousness, numbering in the hundreds of thousands across the country. In fact, "polls taken March 18–23, 1965, showed that the American public favored the Voting Rights Act by a margin of 76 to 16 percent" (Kotz, 2005, p. 314).

The power of the one to affect change in the many is central to the Jungian opus. Jung (1964/1970) discussed the reciprocal power between the individual and culture in his book, *The Undiscovered Self*:

> If the individual is not truly regenerated in spirit, society cannot be either, for society is the sum total of individuals in need of redemption (para. 293) ... What does lie within our reach ... is the change in individuals who have, or create for themselves, an opportunity to influence others of like mind. I do not mean by persuading or preaching—I am thinking, rather, of the well-known fact that anyone who has insight into his own actions, and has thus found access to the unconscious, involuntarily exercises an influence on his environment. (para. 295)

Consciousness develops in direct relationship with one's ability to see and hold the opposites within. Edinger (1995) discussed the importance of developing personal consciousness as an elixir for changing consciousness in the collective:

> You see, these individuals with insight into their own actions, who are aware of the operation of the opposites within themselves, have, to a greater or lesser extent, experienced the coniunctio—the subject matter of the *Mysterium*. Such people, then, are conscious carriers of the opposites. And, to the extent that such individuals exist and carry the opposites within themselves, they do not feed the exteriorization of the terrible strife between the opposites. (Edinger, 1995, p. 325)

In other words, the more one can hold the tension of the opposites, the less likely it is that the outer world will manifest in a split. As the bridge signifies the union of opposites of a once racially divided American South, so the bridge also represents the intrapsychic bridging of the conscious to unconscious forces—good to evil, right to wrong. The paradigm of wholeness was thus constellated in a moment in time.

King taught that to suffer the evil within ourselves enables tolerance in the other and even love. Crossing the bridge from blinding hubris to a union with shadow as a condition of one's nature imbues one with humility, understanding, and, ultimately, the capacity to forgive. No longer do the violent waters of hatred hold the same meaning and power, because one becomes aware of one's part in the problem. Jung (1958) presented his point of view as follows:

> Self-reflection or—what comes to the same thing—the urge to individuation gathers together what is scattered and multifarious, and exalts it to the original form of the One, the Primordial Man. In this way our existence as separate beings, our former ego nature is abolished, the circle of

consciousness is widened, and because the paradoxes have been made conscious, the sources of conflict are dried up. (para. 401)

The march wound its way through Montgomery and ended on the steps of the capital. An epoch of slavery amemliorated where it all began generations ago—this enantiodromia was defining an evolutionary cycle of psychic development. King (2001), in his book, *A Call to Conscience*, aptly described the effects of the marches and this seminal moment of consciousness in the American narrative:

> Selma, Alabama, became a shining moment in the conscience of man. If the worst in American life lurked in its darkest streets, the best of American instincts arose passionately from across the nation to overcome it. There never was a moment in American history more honorable and more inspiring than the pilgrimage of clergymen and laymen of every race and faith pouring into Selma to face danger at the side of its embattled Negros. (p. 121)

Unfortunately, the moment of liberation in Montgomery would not last long, for just hours after King's speech, Viola Liuzzo, a volunteer, would be shot by members of the KKK while driving marchers back to Selma from Montgomery. The death of Mrs. Liuzzo symbolized another cycle of violence moving through the collective, which would continue for months to come as riots broke out across the country. Although the march in Selma achieved a newly adaptive cultural position toward ending racism through the right to vote, the state of consciousness was to be short lived. The marches allowed for just four days of nonviolent quiescence before the Watts Riots exploded in California, seemingly flying in the face of all that had been achieved in the movement since Montgomery.

Nonviolence provided an opening into the center of the complex of racism, exposing America to a truth it could not see or did not want to accept. King's induction of nonviolence into the American psyche allowed the collective to experience its potential for unity and healing through agapeic shadow integration, which, prior to King, had not been experienced en masse in quite the same way. The intersection between nonviolent activism and Jungian analytical psychology provides essential systems of thought that demand further exploration in the greening of the personality and the development of culture.

References

Archive for the Research in Archetypal Symbolism. The Book of Symbols Reflections on Archetypal Images. (2010). Cologne: Taschen Publications.

Combs, B. (2014). *From Selma to Montgomery: The Long Ride to Freedom.* London, New York: Routledge.

Edinger, E. F. (1995). *The Mysterium Lectures: a Journey through C.G. Jung's Mysterium Coniunctionis.* Toronto: Inner City Books.

Fager, C. (1974). *Selma 1965: The March that Changed the South.* New York: Charles Schribner's and Sons.

Ferenczi, S. (2018). "Confusion of Tongues between Adults and the Child" in Michael Balint (ed.), *Final Contributions to the Problems and Methods of Psychoanalysis.* New York: Routledge.

Garrow, D. (1978). *Protest at Selma Martin Luther King Jr., and the Voting Rights Act of 1965.* New Haven, London: Yale University Press.

Ghaemi, N. (2011). *A First-Rate Madness.* London: Penguin Books.

Jung, C. (1958). *Psychology & Religion: West and East. The Collected Works of C.G. Jung* (Vol 11). (W. McGuire, Ed.). Princeton: Princeton University Press.

Jung, C. (1964/1970). *The Undiscovered Self.* Princeton: Princeton University Press.

Kotz, N. (2005). *Judgment Days.* Boston, New York: Houghton Mifflin Company.

King, Jr., Martin Luther (1965). Meet the Press, *NBC News.* (N.Y. Tom Wickert, Interviewer).

King, Jr., Martin Luther (2001). *A Call to Conscience, Edited by Clayborne Carson and Kris Shepard.* New York: Time Warner Book Group.

King, Jr., Martin Luther (2007). *The Papers of Martin Luther King, Jr. Volume VI: Advocate of the Social Gospel.* Berkley Los Angeles London: University of California Press.

Kurlansky, M. (2006). *Nonviolence: the History of a Dangerous Idea.* New York: Random House Publications.

Montiel, C. J. and Christie, D. J. (2008). Conceptual Frame for a Psychology of Nonviolent Democratic Transitions: Positioning Across Analytical Layers. In N. L. R. Hame, *Global Conflict Resolution Through Positioning Analysis* (pp. 261–280). New York: Springer Publications.

Neumann, E. (1969/1990). *Depth Psychology and a New Ethic.* Boston: Shambala Publications.

Samuels, A. (1993/2001). *The Political Psyche.* London, New York: Routledge Publications.

Samuels, A., Shorter, B. and Plant, A. (1986). *A Critical Dictionary of Jungian Analysis.* Routledge: London New York.

Singer, T. and Kaplinsky, C. (2010) "Cultural Complexes in Analysis" in *Jungian Psychoanalysis: Working in the Spirit of C.G. Jung*, Murry Stein (ed). Chicago: Open Court Press.

Singer, T. and Kimbles, S. (2004). *The Cultural Complex.* London, New York: Routledge.

Sidoli, M. (1993). When the meaning gets lost in the body: Psychosomatic disturbances as a failure of the transcendent function. *Journal of Analytic Psychology,* (8): 175–190.

Timm, J. (2019, December 28). "Gerrymandering is alive and well. The coming battle will be bigger than ever." *NBCnews.com.* Retrieved from https://www.nbcnews.com/politics/2020-election/gerrymandering-alive-well-coming-battle-will-be-bigger-ever-n1106951.

Chapter 8

The analytic stance and the eightfold path of nonviolence

By the time the patient arrives in the consulting room, they may have likely endured years of suffering from an oppressive inner other whom they are convinced lives outside of themselves. It is a suffering so engrained that the patient has yet to define him- or herself as a person of free will, able to individuate from and in relation to their personal shadow. The desire to end the oppressive experience can launch the individual on a journey of activism, an inner pilgrimage to a more conscious, meaningful life.

Similar to the practice of nonviolent activism, the analytic process is a dynamic experience of individuation shaped by the two individuals participating in the process. Nonviolence arises organically as a result of the psychological and emotional tension emerging through the transference and countertransference experiences between and within the couple. Through the implementation of the tenets, the instinctual urge to power informed through aggression may be transformed into a state of love and understanding through the process of shadow integration, in one or both parties. According to Gandhi (1962),

> the force of love ... truly comes into play only when it meets with the causes of hatred. True nonviolence does not ignore or blind itself to causes of hatred, but despite the knowledge of their existence, operates upon the person setting those causes in motion. (p. 171)

The analytic relationship consists of two individuals invested in the wellbeing of each other and whose relationship forms a temenos, a sacred spiritual domain. The creative process, called analysis, unfolds as uniquely as the individuals involved; however, the analyst is informed of the experience through training and time and understands that the process must be contained by a structure consisting of boundaries—practical, psychological, and emotional.

At the core of any analysis is relationship building, which is brought to bear on both parties through the discovery of one's self, which emerges through moment-to-moment encounters with the other in the analytic hour.

The inner other consists of unconscious, subjective psychological and emotional experiences shaped by object relations and affected by culture, class, race, religion, and sexual or gender identity. Davies (2011) explained, "The challenge of authentically knowing our patients, or ourselves, is immense. Whether culturally or racially similar or different, we are each subjectively unique, and encountering 'otherness' is therefore central to the analytic endeavor" (p. 550). Holding these differences invariably brings conflict and is an essential element of coming to an understanding of one another and the process of inner knowing. Davies further observed,

> In psychoanalysis, it appears that the *effort* to connect with the 'other' is as psychologically transforming to both participants as the achievement of understanding. The *process* of trying to apprehend the subjectivity of another is complex, unpredictable, and when successful is inevitably altering to both patient and analyst. (p. 550)

Both the *effort* and *process* comprise a form of nonviolent activism, a dynamic of coming into being with one's self through the process of individuation as it occurs in the analytic experience.

Jungian analyst Murray Stein (2006) wrote,

> [Individuation] is a project of consciousness-raising and development, to put it in the simplest possible way. This entails forming a conscious relationship to the various aspects of one's personality not by further identifying with the most prominent features ... but rather by containing all of them maximally within consciousness precisely without such identification. (p. 4)

Individuation, Stein surmised, occurs in two sweeping psychological movements. The first is the dissolution of the ego, via the peeling back of shadow projections. This move involves "separating the pieces of the tangled web of motives and part-selves that constitute our psyche and making the parts more distinct—in other words, struggling with one's character and gaining some distance from it" (p. 6). The second occurs concomitantly when developing a relationship with the Self, which entails "embracing all facets of the Self with a degree of acceptance and respect" (p. 6). Relative to this dual process, according to Stein, "Jungian psychology offers ... a method for holding the paradoxes of the psyche in consciousness and coming to terms with its complexity" (p. 6). To suffer the paradoxes is similar to Gandhi and King's philosophy of nonviolence.

For Gandhi, to achieve complete nonviolence, one would not "become a saint," but instead would become a "true man" (Kurlansky, 2006, p. 8); likewise, the analytic opus contains the seeking of the full human experience through one's relationship with the other. Relationships are complex laden

and imbued with psychological splits, holes in the psyche formed of aggression, which interrupt one's capacity for relatedness. In the suffering of a split,
one rejects the badness in oneself, by projecting out onto another the
unbearable bad parts. Splits then are shaped into all-good or all-bad experiences. Psychological health involves the consistent pursuit of uncovering our
splits and developing the capacity to hold the good and the bad together. The
process is an ongoing psychological task of adult development.

Jung's writings addressed the difficulty of undertaking an analysis and the
suffering of turbulent emotional experiences that can consume the therapeutic
couple. Jungian analyst Pamela Power (2014) iterated, "Whether one calls it
shadow, trauma, resistance, destructiveness, envy, or narcissism, we [analysts]
recognize that when we invite the forces for psychological growth, integration
and individuation to manifest, we also invite the forces of anti-growth, anti-
individuation and anti-life" (p. 33). On a cultural level, the containment and
transformation of aggression and violence is equally, if not more challenging,
as that which the civil rights movement demonstrated, because its implementation threatens homeostasis and calls up from the unconscious shadow
forces that challenge the call for a new moral order. It is the creation of the
temenos and its viability that plays a critical role in the alchemical
transformation of aggression and violence.

The word "*satyagraha* derives from the Hindu word *Satya,* meaning
'truth.' *Satyagraha,* according to Gandhi, literally means 'holding on to truth'
or 'truth-force'" (Kurlansky, 2006, p. 7). The practice of *satyagraha* reflects
the analyst's active commitment to a conscious life or life of self-awareness.
Consciousness involves the practitioner's consistent self-examination, including the level to which aggression and violence have affected their own internal
states as well as the lives of those around them.

Satyagraha cannot be achieved on any level, however, without shadow
integration, or a coming to terms with the hidden, more destructive sides of
the personality. Without nonjudgmental acceptance, shadow remains hidden
from view, and although the work of the shadow complex involves facing
painful hidden truths, the truth serves as the path to wholeness.

In analysis, the analyst must maintain a vigilant watch on the psychic
activity arising from the patient's unconscious. The active pursuit of truth
requires the holding of the tension of opposite forces, both conscious and
unconscious, which can be quite painstaking and turbulent. According to
Gandhi (1993), "nonviolent resistance should reject not only all recourse to
violence but also mere passivity so as to play an active, forceful, even militant
role" (p. xii). The analyst as *satyagrahi* provides a form of psychological
containment from which trust burgeons. Based on human rights advocate
Fabrizio Petri's (2014) analysis of the principle of *satyagraha* as practiced by
Gandhi, this is a feminine practice, an open acceptance of the patient and all
that they bring into the analysis. Petri emphasized, "It is this attitude of the
satyagrahi, of ethical, spiritual and psychological openness—something

extremely difficult to attain and, even more, to maintain—that introduces us to the most important point" (p. 9), which is that *satyagraha* lays the groundwork for the redemption of the feminine (anima development), both individually and collectively (p. 10).

Ahimsa, which means no harm, is derived from the word *himsa*, "to harm," and was defined by Gandhi as "love force" (Kurlansky, 2006, p. 7). *Ahimsa* is the practice of choosing nonviolence over violence, in thought, word, and deed. The transmutation of violence occurs through one's capacity to consciously and reflectively hold aggression while choosing not to act aggressively. *Ahimsa*, according to Gandhi, means "to innovate entirely without revolution; and to deeply transform the present without disregarding the past" (Petri, 2014, p. 8). The practice of *ahimsa*, then, creates space for reconstruction when unconscious enactments constellate potentially destructive projective material. *Ahimsa* is a dedication to love and relationship in the face of aggression.

The analytic relationship imbued with *satyagraha* and *ahimsa* forms a reverie from which the mystery of the wounded ego-Self relationship can emerge. Through moments of meeting, the patient feels seen and experienced by the analyst. These are primary experiences the patient has longed for in the face of their suffering. As Jung (1961/1963) stated, "the patient who comes to us has a story that is not told, and which as a rule no one knows of ... It is a patient's secret, the rock against which he is shattered" (p. 117). Jungian analyst Judith Pickering (2012) described the analyst's job as one of witnessing and suffering with the patient and, in so doing, "to bear witness to the suffering of our patients' ancestors as well as to the suffering that the ancestors may have inflicted on others" (p. 577). She wrote,

> As analysts, we share in bearing unbearable burdens of pain that our patients unwittingly inherit. Through the transformational containment of the analytic relationship, both analyst and patient may begin to think the unthinkable, dream it into conscious awareness and find language to describe what was once indescribable. (p. 577)

It is within the folds of the process and practice of *satyagraha* and *ahimsa* that the imagination comes alive, providing the imagery necessary for personal wellness, obtained through this feminine-based practice. The feminine aspects of *satyagraha* and *ahimsa* sitting beside King's six tenets encourage shadow integration and the unfolding of the other in the analytic experience. Together, these tenets comprise the eightfold path of nonviolence. In his book *Stride Towards Freedom*, King (1958) laid out the tenets of nonviolence as he practiced them.

King's (1958) first tenet states, **"Nonviolence is not passive nonresistance to evil; it is active nonviolent resistance to evil"** (p. 90). As a *satyagrahi*, King stated that active nonviolent resistance "is not a method of stagnant passivity" and explained, "For while the nonviolent resister is passive in the sense that he is not physically aggressive toward his opponent, his mind and emotions are always active, constantly seeking to persuade his opponent that he is wrong" (p. 90). King found a considerable difference between pacifism and activism. He wrote,

> My study of Gandhi convinced me that true pacifism is not nonresistance to evil, but nonviolent resistance to evil. Between the two positions, there is a world of difference ... True pacifism is not in realistic submission to evil ... It is rather a courageous confrontation of evil by the power of love, in the faith that it is better to be the recipient of violence than the inflictor of it, since the latter only multiplies the existence of violence and bitterness in the universe, while the former may develop a sense of shame in the opponent, and thereby bring about a transformation and change of heart. (p. 86)

In terms of an individual's path of transformation, the instinctual urge of individuation sets in motion volatile unconscious psychic forces seeking expression, impinging upon consciousness. These violent forces may arise naturally, developmentally, or they may be constellated by trauma and loss. Either way, individuation demands a new adaptive attitude, one in which one must come to terms with the Self's demands upon one's ego.

Personal activism tends to reflect the political culture as well, as the civil rights movement aptly demonstrated. In terms of what is discovered in psychotherapy, training analyst Adrienne Harris (2007) reported,

> We always find in the patient a conflict which, at a certain point is connected with the great problems of society. Hence, when the analysis is pushed to this point, the apparently individual conflict of the patient is revealed as a universal conflict of his environment and epoch. (p. 137)

Psychoanalyst and object relation theorist Ronald Fairbairn (1935) contended that "all sociological problems are ultimately reducible to problems of individual psychology" (p. 221). Jungian analyst Andrew Samuels (1993), writes extensively on the political psyche, stated,

> The political tasks of modern democracy are similar to the psychological tasks of modern therapy and analysis. In both areas, there is a fight between consciousness, liberation and alterity on the one hand and suppression, repression and omnipotent beliefs in final truths on the other. Psychological and political processes share an uncertain outcome. Hence, the demarcation between the inner world of psychology and the outer world of politics has no permanent existence. The *umwelt* is both inside and outside. (p. 4)

Gandhi and King agreed that nonviolent action was the key to a nonviolent revolution. If one had to act violently, this was a better alternative than pacifism. Gandhi declared,

> My creed of nonviolence is an extremely active force. It has no room for cowardice or even weakness. There is hope for a violent man to be some day non-violent, but there is none for a coward. I have, therefore said more than once … that, if we do not know how to defend ourselves, our women and our places of worship by the force of suffering, i.e., non-violence, we must, if we are men, be at least able to defend all these by fighting (as cited in Ghaemi, 2011, p. 110).

Psychiatrist Nassir Ghaemi (2011) commented that for King, "nonviolence did not mean the absence of violence, but the control of violence so that it was directed inward rather than outward" (p. 109). Nonviolence is a form of spiritual warfare, where violent actions or urges to power are experienced but not acted upon; instead, aggression is *consciously* experienced, contained, and challenged through nonviolent interventions. The real question is how to hold aggression without becoming violent, even long after the initial experience has subsided. Pacifism opens the door to unmediated archetypal forces, and in psychoanalysis, leaves the analyst exposed to the very unconscious forces that have consumed the analysand. Jung (1966) aptly stated,

> Our patients suffer from bondage to a neurosis, they are prisoners of the unconscious, and if we attempt to penetrate with understanding into that realm of unconscious forces, we have to defend ourselves against the same influences to which our patients have succumbed. Like doctors who treat epidemic diseases, we expose ourselves to the powers that threaten our conscious equilibrium and we have to take every possible precaution if we want to rescue not only our own humanity but that of the patient from the clutches of the unconscious. (para.182)

In psychoanalysis, moments of aliveness and ambivalence in the subjectively shared phenomenon known as the *analytic third* are shaped by the transference and countertransference experiences of the participants. Revealed in the form of projection, the transference is an "unconscious emotional bond that arises in the analysand toward the analyst" (Sharp, 1991, p. 136), whereas countertransference is a projection of the "unconscious emotional response of the analyst to analysand" (Sharp, 1991, p. 44). These projective experiences serve as jumping-off points into what will become fertile ground for the patient/activist's demonstrations, infused with shadow material informed by early attachment experiences, group dynamics (social and cultural), and instinctual urges of power and aggression (Dalal, 2006, p. 133). It is the responsibility of the analyst to work with the projective experiences and the archetypal material contained therein. Projective material can be highly charged (love and aggression), and the analyst must be prepared to deal with extremes of affect.

In relation to King's (1958) second tenet, **"Nonviolence does not seek to defeat or humiliate the opponent but to win his friendship and understanding"** (p. 90), the analytic relationship is a sacred bond consisting of a trust whose foundation is formed of kinship libido, which surpasses friendship. Kinship libido, or common humanity, and *agape* enforce analytic trust, providing safety for the unconscious upheavals endemic in the work. Moreover, *agape* allows for the very human shadow to emerge through the analytic encounter, first with the analysand in the transference and, later, through a new consciousness, which begins to evolve as the patient comes to understand their shadow as a form of suffering. Humiliating and shaming a person who has waited years to confess in private what they know to be self-harming, loathsome behaviors will only lead to destruction and an urge to power in defense of a vulnerability that has been squashed by the analyst. The analyst must tend to their own inner shaming and humiliating other, so that the patient does not receive the projection and thus trigger suffering within the analyst still in need of conscious care. However, shaming or humiliation emerging from the transference and interpreted by the analyst is part of the process, because the analysand can then discover, through shadow integration, how they enslave themselves and others through destructive inner dialogue.

Jungian analyst and theorist Edward Edinger (1987) stated, "The ego must be *relativized* to make room for the Self. The totality of the Self brings with it the shadow, an encounter with which is always painful humiliation" (p. 91). The face of the inner other is shaped by shadow, with each event adding to its the depth and breadth. Humiliation does not harm the Self but casts into light that which has been suppressed by the ego. The suffering ego is weakened by humiliation, but appropriately strengthened in its encounter with the Self. Indeed, the other within is the bridge to shadow. Jung (1964/1970) asserted,

> No one who does not know himself can know others. And in each of us, there is another who we do not know. He speaks to us in dreams and tells us how differently he sees us from the way we see ourselves. When, therefore, we find ourselves in a difficult situation to which there is no solution, he can sometimes kindle a light that radically alters our attitude—the very attitude that led us into the difficult situation. (para. 325)

The analyst has been trained to understand the fundamental disconnect of the ego from shadow and must exhibit the capacity to provide an environment that can withstand the bids for power that come with shadow integration. According to Solomon (2007), "if such pressure can be contained in the holding environment of the analyst's capacity for *agape*, it is then that, as

Jung stated, the transcendent function may be activated and a solution found" (p. 257). Through *agape*, conflict and difference are made tolerable, binding the couple together and making possible the introduction of the other within, where the transcendent resides.

King's (1958) third tenet states, **"Nonviolence is directed at the forces of evil rather than the persons who happen to be doing the evil"** (p. 91). Critical in the transformation of aggression is condemning destructive behaviors rather than the person. Providing the opportunity for shadow integration allows the patient to reflect (and struggle) with their ego-oriented behavior, while at the same time exposing them to an experience of the Self through a grace-infused moment with the analyst. A person's ability to reflect on their behavior indicates that they have achieved the capacity to discern the other as a separate being, with good and bad parts. In theory, this tenet poses an immense challenge to those who have been the victim of abuse, racism, or scapegoating, for it requires deep moral introspection through shadow work.

For many civil rights workers, this tenet could be tactically implemented by practicing Christian doctrine and following moral leaders like King and his colleagues. The philosophical applications of this tenet prove exceedingly difficult in practice, however, because supplicating to and wholly accepting the abusive other as an aspect of one's interiority requires more than a cognitive understanding and application. The tenet demands an ongoing commitment to suffering shadow integration through one's relationship with the Self. The suffering of a conscious life for the sake of one's self and the other is the focus of King's fourth and fifth tenets: **"The nonviolent resister is willing to accept violence if necessary but never to inflict it"** (p. 91), and **"avoids not only external violence but also internal violence of spirit"** (p. 92). Although King and his lieutenants trained nonviolent workers to react to violence with nonviolence, this practice was difficult at best, and events such as Bloody Sunday in Selma in 1965 traumatized even those who could hold a nonviolent philosophical stance.

The capacity to hold aggression without destruction to self or other is exceedingly difficult and requires that the practitioner navigate between psychic and somatic experiences mediated by conscious self-reflection and the capacity to hold self–other states. While containment of aggression may enable transformation, there are also significant consequences to one's holding onto aggression without understanding the alchemical process of individuation.

As the Selma demonstrations aptly revealed, events like Bloody Sunday, with the deaths of Jimmie Lee Jackson and James Reeb, made it exceedingly difficult for the workers to hold their aggression in check. Consequently, by the time Turnaround Tuesday rolled around, outbreaks of violence had ensued among the ranks, sometimes between black and white workers. In his book, *A First-Rate Madness*, Ghaemi (2011) wrote that, over time, the effects of suppressing aggression ran deep. Many workers had to be prescribed tranquilizers for unmanageable aggression, causing some to believe that violence was the only cure for racism. Ghaemi relates to psychiatrist Franz Fannon's view that "to overcome psychological servitude, blacks must violently attack their white oppressors" (p. 111), or else unmetabolized aggression threatens to become depression. Ghaemi continued: "Fannon, a favorite of Black Power advocates, saw violence not only as a political necessity but as psychological imperative" (p. 111).

Regarding nonviolence, the question is not *whether* but rather *how* aggression can be adequately expressed with the least amount of trauma or violence. Here is where Fannon and King come together, with King's advocacy of nonviolent activism as the answer, even when it has to be militantly implemented:

> King did not advocate an attitude of peaceful beatitude toward others; he was an angry man, affronted by injustice; he just advocated expressing that anger in a nonviolent way … Rage is a natural part of being human; one cannot deny it without painful psychic consequences. But rage can be channeled in a constructive manner, going outside insofar as it resists injustice, and going inward insofar as it supports the higher courage needed to suffer rather than inflict suffering (Ghaemi, 2011, p. 112).

In analysis, the projection emerges from the throes of aggression, and in the countertransference experience, the analyst must find a way to metabolize the aggression and express, through the unique language only the analytic couple knows, the destructiveness of what is going on. The core of the destructiveness tasks the analyst with the job of fully feeling the aggression, and through self-reflection, patience, and an aptitude for suffering without splitting, wait for the nonviolent tactic to arise; this *is* philosophical nonviolence at work. The culmination of the nonviolent moment may define itself in a tactic such as the sit-in (holding the tension of opposites), singing (exploring breakthroughs), praying (holding of hope), silence (refusal to collude), jailing (suffering of projections), and publicity (an interpretation). The analyst's nonviolent response may collapse the projection, leaving the analysand with a self-reflective choice to integrate the material as an aspect of their own interiority. The emerging consciousness induces organic suffering, integrating ever so slightly the nonviolent activist within. Jungian analyst Ann Ulanov (2001), in her article, "Hate in the Analyst," discussed the importance of the analyst peeling back the projection:

> By disidentifying with our own ego-stance while we still hold it, we see our subjectivity more objectively, which grants the client elbow room to make a wedge between his identifications too. A certain generosity begins to circulate in the field between analysand and analyst that springs from the analyst's own experience of being beheld as an object of attention of a greater subject. The greater subject is the living reality encountered in fresh form. (p. 37)

At some time or another in the analytic journey, each individual, whether master or slave, must recognize the other and comprehend their mutual dependency as their interdependent states of relatedness slide back and forth, titrated by aggression (domination) and love (submission). The analyst's capacity to hold the tension of aggression during the shapeshifting of roles between master and slave is nonviolent activism; however, there are times when the analyst's skills may not be enough to contain aggression that threatens the integrity of the relationship.

When emotional violence becomes habitual in analysis, there may be something deeper at work in the relationship. Jung (1931/1970) discussed the very powerful unconscious bond that initially joins the couple together in a state of near oneness as *"participation mystique"* (para. 203). Developed by French anthropologist Levy Bruhl, *participation mystique* refers to a state in which "the subject cannot clearly distinguish himself from the object" (Power, 2014, p. 35), for the analytic couple's attachment is formed from a "mystical identity, due to the activation of vital, primitive aspects of the psyche. The identity appears as an *a priori* condition, an initial identification that must undergo differentiation—as if for the first time" (Power, 2014, p. 35). The process of separation and differentiation may be exceedingly painful and tortuous for the patient.

At this earliest stage of consciousness, the phenomenon of *participation mystique* "is raw, unreflective experience, practically not yet even conscious, certainly not reflectively so" (Stein, 1995, p. 8). The analyst can recognize this stage of consciousness in many ways, one of which is persistent conflict fueled by envy, aggression and even hatred in one or both parties. Through reverie, the analyst works to contain the primitive states which may arise. Yet, there are times in which aggression is persistent and threatening to the analytic integrity itself. As King suggested, once hate sets in, nonviolent effectiveness falters, because one or both parties have lost the capacity to negotiate or empathize, essentially foreclosing on the couple's communal ability to heal. According to psychoanalyst Otto Kernberg (1998),

> hatred is the dominant effect of the psychopathology of human aggression—the transformation of rage into the structured intrapsychic relationship between a hateful self and a threatening, hateful and hated object that needs to be controlled, to be made to suffer, to be destroyed. (p. 203)

Once hate enters into the analytic container, corruption of the capacity to experience empathy is affected and indicates that a particular sadomasochism has entered the frame. The stage, then, is set for a challenging, long-term struggle between the patient's ego identifying with the internalized master–slave dynamic and the analyst's attempt to make conscious this pattern and to release the patient's ego from the grip of the destructive forces contained within the split.

The entrance of hatred erodes the container that *satyagraha* and *ahimsa* create, deeply impairing one's capacity to hold the hope and faith that *agape* provides. Where the container may be able to withstand aggression, hatred may destroy it. The analyst's ability to work with their own sadomasochistic tendencies and envy complex is critical in navigating the deeply entrenched woundedness in the other. Power (2014) suggested that the pattern of sado-masochism is present in all relationships, "analytic or otherwise, although it is certainly stronger or more obvious in some" (p. 46). She added,

> The question is whether a sadomasochistic relationship can eventually be put to good use. Perhaps the analytic process gets driven into it; as if through a repetition compulsion, the process seeks something vital, deep, alive, and creative. The knowledge that one must be close to the toxin to be vitally creative, psychologically awake and alive is well-known among artists. (p. 46)

Kernberg (1991) stated that "hatred is not always pathological" (p. 216), but can become so when entrenched. He explained, "As a response to an objective, real danger of physical or pathological destruction, a threat to the survival of oneself and those one loves, hatred is a normal elaboration of rage aimed to eliminate danger" (p. 216). The key for working with hate, then, as King's life aptly demonstrated, depends on "how much lightening we can stand" (Ulanov, 2001, p. 35). Kernberg (1991) asserted, however, that "as a chronic, characterological predisposition, hatred always reflects the psychopathology of aggression" (p. 216). In the face of hate, the split may become calcified unless one or both individuals can find a way back home to each other and within themselves.

The solution to unlocking the sadomasochistic paradigm involves the analyst's capacity to persist nonviolently in ongoing demonstrations, which would confront the patient's inner sadomasochist by refusing its projective identification. Kernberg (1991) commented,

> Obviously, by means of projective identification, the patient is attributing to the therapist his own hatred and sadism, but, by the same token, the total situation illustrates the intimate link between the persecutor and the persecuted, master and slave, sadist and masochist. (p. 226)

In the face of the patient's projections, it is imperative that the analyst stay tuned to their own potential for violence to the patient, fueled by their own capacity to hate.

The patient who achieves the depressive position can experience the analyst as good and bad at the same time. When each survives conflict with the other, the relationship deepens, imbued with a mutually dependent trust of the other. The confidence that is cultivated weakens shadow, illuminating the appropriate inner master–slave (Self-ego) experience—true spiritual freedom. This bridging points the way toward a new dream, an experience that unfurls slowly moving the ego from exile to home.

Ulanov (2001) poignantly stated that the Self is dissolving and creating a force of nature and that analysts must learn to ride these states of deconstruction and construction while the patient discovers themselves (p. 35). To hold, meditate, and relatedly express hurtful feelings is the life-long practice of a *satyagrahi*. Gandhi (1962) emphasized that the capacity to keep one's aggression in check through self-awareness and persistence could transform violence into peace. He revealed, "I have learned through bitter experience, the one supreme lesson to conserve my anger, and as the heat conserved is transmuted into energy, even so our anger controlled can be transmuted into a power which can move the world" (p. xxii). Ulanov (2001) reiterated this idea:

> What I have learned from focusing on hate in the analyst is that without it we cannot find its transformation and we cannot arrive at the vision where even the smallest of things participates in the largest life of the divine. This vision sustains our analytical work over decades, because we can see in the ridiculous complex that still plagues us the beseeching of the divine to reach us. We can see how what appears trivia, and therefore is hatefully scorned, in fact, is the secret doorway to spiritual renewal. (p. 36)

In the complex of racism, when each party can begin to own their projections, repealing their belief that the other is the oppressor, racism becomes the illusion that skin color hides. King (1958) stated that underneath the races lay split souls in need of care, which may only heal through cultural repair, a repair that begins within the one and spreads to the many through the practice of nonviolence. He further specified,

> Since the white man's personality is greatly distorted through segregation, and his soul is greatly scarred, he needs the love of the Negro. The Negro must love the white man, because the white man needs his love to remove his tensions, insecurities and fears. (p. 94)

Nonviolence may not hold all of the answers, but it does provide a pathway into the inner world, where the true source of racism resides, and can, through practice, affect some form of change; to what degree is determined by the depth and breadth of one's capacity for consciousness. When the analysand and analyst can experience the rightful, democratic power paradigm, *agape* becomes the dominant ingredient interdependently intertwining the pair, connecting them to a higher purpose, for the greater good of the community. The experience induces psychological justice, an idea to which King (1958) referred in his sixth tenet: **"Nonviolence is based on the conviction that the universe is on the side of justice"** (p. 95).

King's philosophical idea of justice is similar to Jung's concept of the transcendent function, the symbol-making function of the psyche. According to Jung (1921),

> the symbol always says: in some such form as this a new manifestation of life will become possible, a release from bondage and world-weariness. The libido that is freed from the unconscious by means of the symbol appears as a rejuvenated god, or actually as a new god. (para. 435)

In addition, where King stated that the universe is on the side of justice, Jung (1921) similarly said that the "redeeming symbol is a highway, a way upon which life can move forward without torment and compulsion" (para. 445). Both King and Jung pointed toward a form of psychic justice, or some form of life that is released from the struggle between violence and nonviolence. This is the process of the transcendent level of existence emerging from the Self, Indeed, the Self is always dissolving and creating itself, as is each individual in relationship to self and other, with one inextricably affecting the other and their hermeneutic relationship shaping individual and collective consciousness.

References

Dalal, F. (2006). Racism: Processes of Detachment, Dehumanization, and Hatred. *The Psychoanalytic Quarterly*, 75(1), 131–161.

Davies, J. E. (2011). Cultural Dimensions of Intersubjectivity. *Psychoanalytic Psychology* 28(4), 549–559.

Edinger, E. (1987). *The Christian Archetype A Jungian Commentary on the Life of Christ*. Toronto: Inner City Books.

Fairbairn, R. W. (1936). The Sociological Significance of Communism Considered in the Light of Psycho-Analysis. *The British Journal of Medical Psychology*, 15(3): 218–229.

Gandhi, M. (1962). *The Essential Gandhi*. New York: Vintage Books.

Gandhi, Mohandas K. (1993). *An Autobiography The Story of My Experiments with Truth*. Boston: Beacon Press.

Ghaemi, N. (2011). *A First-rate Madness: Uncovering the Links Between Leadership and Mental Illness*. London: Penguin Books.

Harris, A. (2007). Discussion of Eyal Rozmarin's "An Other in Psychoanalysis." *Contemporary Psychoanalysis*, 43, 361–373.

Jung, C. G. (1921) *The Collected Works of C.G. Jung Psychological Types*, Volume 6. New Jersey: Princeton University Press.

Jung, C. G. (1956). *The Collected Works of C.G. Jung*, Volume 5, Symbols of Transformation, Bollingen Series. Princeton: Princeton University Press.

Jung, C. (1964/1970). *The Collected Works of C.G. Jung Volume 10, Civilization in Transition*. Princeton: Princeton University Press.

Jung, C. (1966). *The Collected Works of C.G. Jung, Volume 16, The Practice of Psychotherapy*. Princeton: Princeton University Press.

Jung, C. G. and Jaffe, Aniela (ed.) (1961/1963) *Memories, Dreams Reflections.* New York, Toronto: Random House Publications.

Kernberg, O. (1991). The Psychopathology of Hatred. *Journal of American Psychoanalytic Association*, 39s, 209–238.

Kernberg, O. F. (1998). Aggression, Hatred, and Social Violence. *Canadian Journal of Psychoanalysis*, 6 (2): 191–206.

King Jr, M. L. (1958). *Stride Toward Freedom.* Boston: Beacon Press.

Kurlansky, Mark (2006). *Nonviolence: The History of a Dangerous Idea.* New York: Random House Publishing.

Petri, F. (Summer 2014, Vol. 41:1). Gandhi, Jung and Nonviolence Today The Relevance of the Feminine in the Network Society. *IIC Quarterly*, 7–18.

Pickering, J. (2012). Ancestral Transmission Through Dreams and Moving Metaphors. *The Journal of Analytical Psychology*, 57(5), 576–596.

Power, P. J. (2014). "Negative Coniunctio" Envy and Sadomasochism in Analysis in *Shared Realities*, Ed. Mark Winborn. Shaitook: Fisher King Press.

Sala, H. (2014, December 17). The Door of Reconciliation. Retrieved from https://www.guidelines.org/devotional/the-door-of-reconciliation/.

Samuels, A. (1993). *The Political Psyche.* New York: Routledge.

Sharp, D. (1991). *C.G. Jung Lexicon A Primer of Terms & Concepts.* Toronto: Inner City Books.

Solomon, H. M. (2007). *The Self in Transformation.* London: Karnac.

Stein, M. (1995). *Encountering Jung: Jung on Evil, Selected and Introduced by Murray Stein.* Princeton: Princeton University Press.

Stein, M. (2006). *The Principle of Individuation Toward the Development of Human Consciousness.* Wilmette: Chiron Publications.

Ulanov, A. (2001). Hate in the Analyst. *Journal of Jungian Theory and Practice* 3, 25–40.

Whitney, M. (Director). (1986). *Matter of Heart* [Motion Picture].

Chapter 9

The case of Linda

She sits on the couch as erect as a proud bird. She is smiling ear to ear: "Well, I did it. I just had to do it. I was compelled by something inside that just wouldn't let me rest until I did it. And, now, I love it. I'm glad I did it, I feel so liberated!" I'm elated. I don't think I've ever seen Linda so pleased with herself. She's finally done something on her own without the jaw-grinding agony of seeking permission from her inner captor.

Linda is speaking of her new shiny, bald head which used to be adorned by soft, flowing gray curls. Spontaneously moved by an inner joy at the lifting of her long-standing depression, she has shaved her head. New earrings adorn her lobes, bobbing in time to the rhythm of her head which is rocking back and forth, springing up and down as she laughs. Indeed, it has been a steep road for her. Nine years of treatment and much suffering from a depression she has been running from since early childhood.

I wonder about the shaving of the head. I wonder if initiation is at hand, the act signaling the crossing of a threshold to a spiritual deepening. I am intrigued and curious about what is being exposed and presaged for the next phase of the work. She has been introduced to sides of herself which she understands to be violent, destructive and wounding to those around her, as well as to herself. The shadow of her personality shows itself in the power struggle, which first takes place inside of her and then is projected out and into personal and professional relationships, and, of course, with me.

At some point in this power-infused dynamic, a crisis may offer itself up as a sacrifice for peace. Peace can be won at the expense of an inner power struggle, a long-standing relational pattern formed from a psychological split embedded within the patient's psyche and which must be excavated in the analytic experience for the patient to be freed from a life of servitude to the internalized master–slave, other. Any discussion of the master–slave paradigm in this case or book is not meant to demean, dismiss, or fundamentally diminish the suffering of the African American experience of slavery; a form of suffering that I could never know as a white person. However, the term master–slave is utilized to portray a fundamental archetypal psychic split universally experienced as the master–slave, a form of oppression. The archetypal master–slave pattern may very well be the original experience of suffering in the human soul, nature's psychic birthmark. The split initiates the soul's experience shapeshifting into different complexes as the psyche evolves. The healing of the split(s) occurs through a relationship of trust, one that allows for the transformational properties of life to take hold, re-building for the individual an inner world in which the soul can survive and possibly thrive. For Linda, the master–slave has ruled her inner life, creating extensive suffering as she has struggled to become her own person. As she sits talking about how much better she feels, my mind's eye travels back in time to the first time I ever met her....

Linda enters the consulting room; her shoulders slumped, her gait slow. The burden of a life riddled from abuse and neglect is evidenced in her tiny frame which has been cursed by chronic fatigue, a trademark of her victimhood. And while Linda is not African American, as a gay woman she has been oppressed and marginalized most of her life.

She avoids making eye contact. I have learned over the years this means she has had a bad day, one of the unrelated, hostile kind. We both have histories of trauma, those injuries that never really heal. Nonviolence enables me to tether myself to an ongoing struggle to understand hatred and oppression, as well as its ugly permutations, especially as they reside in me. I know that in practicing my own nonviolence I must refuse to act out in equal measure when the patient's traumas are ripped open and exposed, threatening their sense of wellbeing. Unfortunately, sometimes a re-exposure to the trauma is the necessity for the relief of suffering. Some days involve an unbearable agony for both of us, but Linda challenges me and teaches me, as I attempt to understand her inner violent nature, while helping her to become an advocate for her own life.

The session begins with the general audit report of her week, which is laced with a particular resentment towards her inner captors, those established self-destructive defenses, for having kept her confined to a life of professional servitude, defined by an oppressive work ethic, driven by her negative animus. Linda is a professional accountant. "I hate people," she tells me early on in the work, "and I'm sure they don't like me either." While her job demands meticulous attention, she often works into the evenings and on weekends in order to get the job done—according to her standards. I wonder about her ability to fully concentrate on the task at hand, due to her dissociative tendencies, a consequence of the trauma she suffered as a child. Her more than rigorous work ethic is highly concerning to me and reflects her defense against the depression that has haunted her most of her life, revealing the inner master who drives her deeply into herself, often locking her away from human relationships, into a world she has tricked herself into believing is safe. Sadly, this false sense of safety has finally turned on her.

When Linda arrives for her initial consult, her depression is raging, grinding her psyche to a screeching halt. I find her in the waiting room, deeply distressed, her depression evidenced by her inability to stop crying or put into words the experience by which she is overwhelmed. Her despair, fueled by free-floating anxiety, keeps her body charged and agitated. She finds relief from this agitation through excessive exercise, sometimes for several hours every day. On this particular day, she sits rocking from side to side in an attempt to soothe herself. For most of the initial consult, Linda does not talk. There are no words for the dread that haunts her.

The first eight months of treatment take on a particular rhythm which forms the container within which Linda can deposit her existential anxieties. Soon, I am able to dialogue with her inner figures, but not before much more anamnesis and stabilization. I'm grateful and relieved when she feels safe enough to bring in a dream.

When a patient discloses a dream, it indicates that he or she feels safe enough to share a very private, intimate side of him- or herself to the analyst. The bridge of trust established in the analysis also signals that a vital link has been made within the patient, for it creates a gateway for the symbolic language of the soul which reveals itself through the dream. According to Jung,

> The dream is a little hidden door in the innermost and most secret recesses of the soul, opening into the cosmic night which was psyche long before there was any ego-consciousness, and which will remain psyche no matter how far out ego-consciousness extends (Jung, 1964/1970, para. 304).

The dream doorway is the connection to the sacred mystery of that which heals. The dream is the link to the Self.

The dream connects the waking and sleeping realms providing the patient with the total experience of their world, showing "the inner truth and reality of the patient as it really is: not as I (the analyst) conjecture it to be, and not as he would like it to be, but *as it is*" (Jung, 1966, para. 304). Through the dream, the patient's true reality or psychic reality emerges, and this provides the individual with truth about themselves they may otherwise not know and informs the next step on the journey to psychological wholeness. It is the underground railroad that will lead the patient out of slavery, one step at a time. Linda's dream reveals the agony of her depression:

> *I am watching a small child, around one year old, crawl over big boulders. She has on a large dirty t-shirt which she drags behind her. It is dark and stormy out. She is trying to stay ahead of a dark cloud coming towards her from behind.*

Linda observes her infantile self from a distance. She is overcome with sadness, despair and worry for the wellbeing of the child. The clouds hold the affect for the wordless dread that she experiences when she is depressed.

The clouds are the depression which threatens to haunt her throughout her life; the clouds construct the original image from which the appearance of the inner other will emerge. In her adult life, the clouds have become the sadistic inner master who drives Linda into a professional world defined by perfectionism and workaholism, which locks her out of a meaningful life. However, it is through the doorway of the shadow that a new rightful loving master can emerge to lead her out of isolation and loneliness.

Through nonviolent activism Linda will come to understand that the master–slave is not a fixed pattern of victimization but is a dynamism whose origins are rooted within the collective unconscious, accessed through the dream and converted into consciousness through shadow integration. It is through the analysis that the mystery of her soulful existence becomes known giving life to a new dream for her life, happening within her and between the two of us, changing, together.

As Linda's initial dream shows, the depression has shaped her, and she will have to undergo tremendous suffering to heal the split developed from abuse. The darkness that encases her in dread has the potential to foreclose on her psychological development. It is a fear that leaves relationships behind, replaced by an urgent need to stay ahead of the terror through a frantically paced workaholism.

Abuse impairs a child's developmental capacities on many levels. Trust, the fundamental building block of all relationships, can be profoundly disrupted. Similar to rickety scaffolding, the traumatized child exists in an inner world defined by insecurity and uncertainty, convinced that one small step in the wrong direction might send them tumbling into an emotional void, never to be caught and contained by a secure inner parent.

From trauma's epicenter, neuropathways to healthy brain development become impaired, whereby virtual roadblocks are erected hampering the child's emotional regulation, verbal acuity, and organized thinking. Trauma forms a wound that bores through the physical realm down into the victim's spiritual experience of life creating a psychological split(s). The trauma can have severe consequences because the child is ill-equipped to cope with the experience. Jungian analyst Donald Kalsched, in his book *Trauma and the Soul: A Psychospiritual Approach to Human Development and Its Interruption* explains:

> An infant or young child who is abused, violated or seriously neglected by a caretaking adult is overwhelmed by the intolerable affects that are impossible for it to metabolize, much less understand or even think about. A shock to the psychosomatic unity of the personality threatens to shatter the child to its very core-threatens to extinguish that 'vital spark' of the person so crucial for the experience of aliveness and so central to the later experience of 'feeling real.' Such a shattering would be an unimaginable catastrophe (2013, p. 11).

Because trauma by its very nature is feeling oriented, it is through the feeling function that the blast of the explosion is initially experienced. And, it is into the blowhole of the trauma that the analytic couple must descend, the patient recovering the vital part of themselves that has gone into self-protective hiding from the trauma (Kalsched, 2013). If the child is born into an existence defined by transgenerational trauma, they bear the burden of the generational trauma plus their individual suffering. These deep psychic wounds shape a dynamic inner life defined by various patterns of resistance; the soul imprisoned by an internal division, one side of the split enslaving the other, thus giving birth to the master–slave within.

The delicate nature of the initial weeks of treatment takes the shape of a slow, rhythmic, rocking. Linda longs to be seen, deeply understood and experienced as a whole person with her thoughts, feelings, dreams, and desires. She is seeking out someone to trust who can actively advocate for her. The crucible of the work is formed of *Satyagraha* and *Ahimsa*: my analytic devotion to the pursuit of consciousness, and dedication to nonviolence. I understand that in the individuation process, nonviolence takes many forms. Sometimes, a particular emotional violence may be the only force that creates a new consciousness. It crashes through old walls with the force of a tank, shocking the patient, but tipping over their old, outdated structures while they are being forced to look.

Historically, Linda's depression and her tendency to run from her terror-filled inner world have contributed to a life defined by work. Her workaholic tendencies are an enactment of the internal master who drives her to distraction and buries her in a voiceless despondency which occupies a large part of the initial sessions. She has been trained to react passively to life in the face of inner and outer violence. The wordless dread which shapes the oppression that bites deeply into her entrenched work ethic baring the markings of a slave sprinting towards a freedom she may never know, but which she works frantically to find.

The life Linda is forever seeking lies right in front of her, but she is unaware of its attainability. She has always felt as if she lives in a land of the forgotten, feeling misunderstood and lost. She lives in a marginalized world, separated from the rest of humanity waiting to be rescued. This archetypal experience of the exile is explained more thoroughly when, one day, Linda confesses that she is gay. She unfurls the long and painful story of her journey to become fully, sexually herself. The discovery comes at a high price, personally and professionally, losing one job because of it, her deep-seated anxiety with work suddenly becoming evident. The traumas of Linda's life fill in many of the blanks that the depression absorbs as I begin to understand why she feels that she "disappears" in her job, with sometimes hours passing before she realizes that the sun has lowered in the sky, or the office is emptied of workers who have left for the day. Her relationship with time helps me to see that she is chaotically organized, held together by an overactive imagination which acts as the binding agent for her mind. It is safe for Linda to lock the outer world away while silently dialoguing with imaginary inner characters. This fantasy world holds her hostage so that each time she is called to consciousness by the demands of her life she is seduced back into the imaginative realm through something we both come to understand as her rescue fantasies, which emerge through humor.

Linda loves numbers, and when she is anxious she talks at length about algorithms, balance sheets and demanding clients and their timelines. I attempt to break through her defensive walls with curiosity about the numbers and what they mean to her. I tend to rely on spontaneity and humor, an essential tactical nonviolent move, which she initially meets with silence and a look of confusion. As her worrying dissolves ever so briefly, she spontaneously burps up a giggle. The humor challenges her obsessive ruminating and the sway it holds over her ego. Through humor a hole forms in the wall of these fortified defenses, giving both of us a glimpse into her very human warmth. Indeed, she realizes she will not be punished for being herself, and suddenly recognizes something spontaneous, playful and innocent within may have left as the depression moved in. When she affirms this observation, she is at once filled with relief at being seen, but also ashamed, because she doesn't know how to change this immovable beast within herself. In this moment of meeting, when our relationship has taken the shape of an intimate kind, my expression assures her not to worry, to let nature take its course, to trust. She carefully examines me. Her stare bores down deeply into me as if to say, "Yeah ... Riiiight, that shit don't happen round here." I hold the moment with a certain subtle confidence in my trust of her. She stares long and hard, critically wondering about me, as if to say, "Who is this woman?" While she does not initially say very much, she remains riveted to my eyes, as if she is fearful I will disappear should she look away. Somewhere in the exchange, the bond of the inner master–slave is slackened ever so slightly, creating space for the emergence of her inner activist. The idea that I take Linda's inner life seriously allows her to open up about her secret world. She recalls that the rescue fantasies have been alive in her mind since the age of four. I wonder if the fantasies began as a response to childhood abuse and the unconscious wish to be rescued in her state of despair and helplessness.

Initially, she is very ambivalent and frightened about disclosing the fantasies which keep her occupied. However, therapy provides an environment in which she can surrender to the hypervigilance that regulates her psychic reality and share her fears with someone. She doesn't understand the fantasies as a reasonable response to trauma, that they form a psychic skin of comfort which the trauma has stripped from her. On the day she decides to trust me enough to break out from the ruminating, a quiet hush falls between us, revealing an opening. I wait. She seems to peak out from behind a hidden veil of secrecy and vulnerability, drawing me to her. I sit silently and wait. She quietly discloses a series of stories that she utilizes to soothe herself in her most worried places. These stories provide her with a sense of relief and comfort, while at the same time engendering guilt, because she understands that these fantasies are unhealthy; they keep her entombed behind a glass wall, yet nevertheless in control. We come to understand these narratives to be a part of her inner hero, who sits at the center of the rescue fantasies. She has been held captive for years, in a world in which she can only dream of being set free.

In these specific narratives, Linda is called in to rescue herself and others from dire living conditions. A typical scenario might unfold as follows: "I am in a forest on a hill, and there is a fire that is threatening to burn the town below. A voice asks, 'How will you put out the fire?' I answer, 'I'll go find the water.' The voice retorts, 'What if you can't find the water?' and I answer, 'Well, I'll use dirt'." The conditions become more and more dire as Linda's resources are tested. She eventually ends up saving her own life, as well as the lives of others, but comes out of the fantasy completely exhausted and having lost all track of time.

In another fantasy, Linda imagines that she walks into a dining room occupied by a family who fulfills her image of happiness. They invite her to come and join them. This experience provides her with a sense of comfort from a world that heretofore has not included her in the human story, a powerful and painful experience of the scapegoated and marginalized. I am touched and moved by Linda's honesty and vulnerability. Although she feels that these fantasies are unproductive, they also reveal a hidden resilience in Linda, the possible wellspring of life which, once accessed, can incarnate the living hero ensconced within her personality, filling in the image of the ghost with a real person. Indeed, her fantasies are steppingstones, the gems that help to uncover the essence to who she is.

I hope that I can help Linda embark upon a nonviolent way of life, one that will bridge to an active nonviolent demonstration. However, her inner master–slave relational pattern is entrenched, her fantasy world an anchor to her suffering, which she is not yet willing to give up. I understand that as the activism takes hold, she will have to deal with an ensuing power dynamism inherent in the master–slave relationship within, and then emerging between the two of us. I get my first peek at her psychic world when she brings in the following dream:

I am in an Israeli sandwich shop with my partner. You are there. The sandwich shop has been given to my partner because the Jewish owner is bankrupt. My partner has taken over the business and is speaking Hebrew to the old owner. The store is flourishing under her care. She is sitting at a table, and you and I are speaking with her. She is crying. I am sitting next to you and feeling like you're making progress with her. And she is talking about something very emotional and vulnerable. Just as I believe she is about to make a break through, you ask her if she is ready to commit or go deeper and she says no. This disappoints me. I wait for these moments when she may somehow be introspective about her own thoughts and feelings.

You are somewhere else in the restaurant when a young girl approaches me; she is African American, around the age of twelve. She sits down in front of me. She asks me to help her with a project on child development. She is working on child development from the ages of zero, infancy, one and two. I attempt to help her with this project.

The Israeli sandwich shop depicts Linda's psychic reality. Her world is defined by oppression, both on a transgenerational level and personal level. The dream also reflects Linda's psychic split. One half is aligned with the treatment and the work, and the other half is working hard to rebuild something that has been lost, resulting in a bankrupt psychological position. The bankrupt owner symbolizes the wound in need of treatment, which is transgenerational, cultural and personal. The healing symbol enters into the dream through the image of the therapist, Linda's developing Self, who offers to join the two sides of the split together through a relationship of vulnerability and communication. Linda's fears and lack of trust in the world in general are reflected in the store owner's ambivalence to go deeper. The ambivalence may also be an aspect of the transference and an unconscious allegiance she has to her defenses, symbolized in her partner.

A break in the action of the dream also indicates a shift in perspective or a descent into another level or area of the dreamer's psyche. It is as if the dreamer has taken herself into the recesses of the split via the introduction of the African American adolescent girl, an important guiding figure. Linda discloses abuse and neglect as a young child and reports a particularly severe trauma at the age of twelve, which has contributed to her deep-seated insecurities about success, competency, and sense of autonomy. The young girl urges Linda to explore these early years of life, which are also laced with trauma. It is as if the guide points the way to the building of a bridge between the fragmented aspects of her psyche thus joining her ego to her Self. Yet, Linda will have to navigate through the striations of her psyche which include transgenerational, cultural and early traumas. The dreamer's life is replete with a sadness that begs to be understood. She longs for a reverie, a place where she can begin to make sense of her traumas, desires and dreams for a more complete life. This will require not just holding and nonviolently containing her resistances and longings, but a relationship which engages Linda in the deeper parts of her personality which have gone into hiding due to the oppressive and abusive conditions of her early life. These oppressive and abusive parts have taken on a life of their own, living within, and rule her inner wheelhouse of agency. Her enslaved other needs to be accessed and integrated for a fuller life.

Aggression, when mediated by strong parents, empowers a child. It strengthens not only the child's ego but ultimately enables her access to the nonviolent aspects of herself. If children can learn that doing bad things does not make them bad and that despite any bad actions, they are lovable, a flexible ego structure develops and subsequently a healthy ego-Self axis as well. Ideally, if individuation proper could have taken hold in the second half of life, Linda would be able to contribute to the world utilizing her capabilities. Unfortunately, Linda had parents with minimal psychological agency. With no parental interventions to mediate the archetypal energies, Linda is annihilated over and over again. Consequently, she exists in a state of constant fear of her rage and her capacity to destroy the other, as well as fear of the other's ability to destroy her. Her fear of annihilation by the other causes an introjection of aggression, creating an inner rage (Benjamin, 1988, p. 53).

Jessica Benjamin (1988) describes the sadomasochistic master and slave dynamic as something developing out of the infant's omnipotence, an affective position that develops out of rage and lack of a safe "other" to contain the experience. With no pushback from the parent, the child develops a sense of omnipotence which evolves into sadism.

> For him, the real object, the one who cannot be destroyed, never comes into view. For him, agency and assertion are not integrated into the context of mutuality and respect for the other but in the context of control and retaliation. (p. 70)

The child might have a cognitive awareness that the mother is separate from her, but is not emotionally integrated enough to understand this fact.

Benjamin (1988) asserts that the parent must be able to hold the child's rage enough that the child develops a sense of limitations between Self and other. The child comes to understand that her anger hurts the other. When she experiences no pushback from the parent, the other disappears and, consequently, she disappears over the edge as well (pp. 50–53). Without my tending to the omnipotence just enough so that Linda could burn off some aggression, she falls into the void in nearly every session, whether disappearing into a fantasy world or becoming entombed in a wordless space of frustration. During these times, Linda would often leave the office by depositing a moment in my lap, which would let me know how angry she was, and then she would leave before we could talk about it. Upon revisiting the moments, she would shirk off the experience as meaningless, accusing me of being overly sensitive, or over-analyzing. The cycle seemed endless until one day, I was finally introduced to the image of that bestial, oppressive inner ruler.

It had been a challenging time at work for Linda. Linda was working at a frenzied pace, driven to distraction at work by relationships in the office which she feels are abusive. And, despite this fact she can't keep herself from returning to the office on the weekends, holidays and even after dinner during the weekdays. She cannot yet verbalize that which is oppressing her, but over time she is able to describe these feelings as dread and doom. Dread and doom visit her just as she begins relaxing at home after a long day's work, or on the weekends, just as she is waking up on Saturday mornings. Deeply unrooted by the feelings, she takes flight in her work, tethering herself to her computer, hating that she is back at work, yet unable to leave. Freedom and enjoyment are flatly forbidden.

Any attempts on my part to push Linda into challenging her unhealthy work ethic are met with tremendous resistance. Indeed, I am witnessing a force of nature within Linda. She locks me out of treatment at the mere hint of confronting her inner professional daemon. One day, while she is exploring the inner depths of her imagination around her daemon, I ask her "who" is forbidding her a life outside of work? In the long pause of silence, Linda looks at me as a child who has stolen their first candy bar, negotiating whether or not to tell, the guilt and fear of retribution palpable. She gambles on trusting me. She looks down momentarily, apparently ready to share her secret: "I'm not allowed to tell," she says. I wait. "You seem really frightened. Why aren't you allowed to tell?" I ask. "It's not safe," she says. I wonder with her, "What will happen if you tell me?" I feel a shift in the time-space continuum within which we live, when suddenly, Linda seems very small. Her body shrivels, receding into the couch as if to make space for something big and menacing. She whispers, "I'll get in big trouble." I ask her who will harm her, and she states, "the witch." Linda and I sit together in silence as if waiting for something to enter the room, which we both have known through the analytic experience, but which, until now, has had no image or voice.

Linda describes the witch as an entity whom she has known all her life, and whom she is terrified of, due to the witch's tendency for retribution. When prompted about what kind of crime she would be punished for, she doesn't know. The witch *is* the master, a psychic entity which haunts her and is a central source of Linda's suffering, and that which keeps her tethered to her fantasy life. The witch fuels her fantasies and stands at the threshold of reality. She consumes a large part of Linda's psychic reality. It is the witch that drives her to distraction in her job and keeps her separated from her relationships. While the witch may be the source of her mother complex, she also contains the roots of the deeper, cruel inner master.

The revelation of the witch provides an important opportunity to begin the process of flipping her life from a largely inner existence to one of being alive in the outer world. However, with the revelation of the witch comes a warning—which I unfortunately ignore. I recall the Israeli sandwich shop dream which shows that she isn't quite ready to commit completely, to trust her capacity to wrestle openly with the inner forces that abuse her. As a result, my pushing for Linda's confrontation with the witch backfires, and she continues to resist any interventions I might suggest. Linda wants to break free from the

oppressive conditions but does not yet feel she will survive on her own without her fantasy life to comfort her. She exists somewhere between the two
worlds of fantasy and reality, attending to her job, hidden from life, locked in
depression. Nevertheless, Linda is brave enough to draw the witch. She
doesn't like to talk about the witch, because she brings so much sorrow and
fear, but through a nonviolent containing, she begins to talk about and
explore the origins of the witch.

My practice of *Ahimsa* and *Satyagraha* allows for the containment of
Linda's fragmented parts through my witnessing without condemnation. I
hold a mirror to the good parts of Linda's nature and eventually, Linda starts
to emerge from hiding. Yet, the truth force of *satyagraha* lays bare the falla-
cies of Linda's fantasy life. Eventually, she can no longer turn away from the
painful truth. Consequently, she begins to become oppositional and defiant in
her need to be in control, and her brittle world begins to crack.

Everyone else in her life is unavailable or unable to understand her. Therefore, she remains isolated at work; alliances fall away due to her need to be in
control, and her projections that everyone else is inadequate. She is that which
she fears but doesn't see. Eventually, I will also become inadequate, inept. Her
opposition is subtle at first; forgetting the check, coming in late, canceling at

Figure 9.1 The Witch

the last minute. Later, she begins to refuse to confront her feelings of helplessness, insisting instead that her helplessness is due to others undervaluing
her and holding her hostage at her job. Her difficulties stem from her boss'
expectations, her co-workers' inadequacies, or work deadlines. She feels like
an object at work, used by others for their betterment. She is but a tool utilized to meet bookkeeping deadlines. She retorts against the suggestion she
could take a well-earned holiday: "You don't get it! I can't go on a vacation.
The business needs me! Besides, no one else can do my job as good as me." I
urge her to discuss her feelings with her boss; she laughs: "Right, like that will
do anything; she is buried in work too." Finally, I attempt to encourage her to
resolve conflict with her co-workers: "Yeah, right, like they care anyway."

Regardless of my attempts to connect with her, she tends to remain stub-
bornly ensconced in an inner position of intolerance for others, victimization,
and defensive hubris, all designed to cover up her fears of failure and inability
to connect with anyone outside of her world of fantasy and work. Soon, her
opposition to me and my attempts at connection begin to wear away at the
analytic alliance, as we both begin trading seats on the *Titanic*, negotiating
the ever-destructive position of power. I start to feel bound up with her witch,
risking becoming witchy myself. The most difficult part of the nonviolent way
is holding the tension of opposites and not giving into my own instinctual
aggression and frustration, but instead, learning to transform the aggression
through the mystery of relationship. Indeed, the trickster was at play, and the
air crackled with an unbearable tension.

Psychoanalyst Jody Messler Davies, in her article "Whose Bad Objects Are
We Anyway? Repetition and Our Elusive Love Affair with Evil," describes
the dangerous and destructive dance of hatred that can ensue in an analytic
relationship with difficult patients, and the shame-filled experiences that each
desperately attempt to avoid, for fear of losing his or her mind. However,
these experiences may be necessary to free the patient from the hellish,
violence-filled chasms within their personality:

> I often find myself feeling that I am engaged in some kind of life and
> death battle for my sanity and mental integrity. I often feel pressed into a
> position in which the only way to affirm a patient's sanity and experience
> of reality is to accept a vision of myself that is so toxic and malignant
> that it feels threatening to my own sense of stability and identity, and I
> begin to feel crazy myself. The presence of a psychotic-parent—of one
> who forced the acceptance of an insane reality as the precondition for a
> loving relationship onto and into a vulnerable child—hovers around the
> consulting room exuding a malignant and sulfurous stench, fueling the
> game of projective-introjective hot potato from which the patient and I
> struggle to emerge intact. There is a desperate frenzy to our struggle, as
> though we are playing the children's card game "Old Maid," in which the
> dark and foreboding queen of spades skulks around the table—inside one

hand and then another, inside me and then you, popping up here and then there: "Not me, I don't want her. Get rid of her; pass her onto someone else. I don't want to be left holding the witch/queen." Perhaps the dilemma in dyadic relationships is simply this: if it is not me, then it must be you. And how do we allow for the presence of such toxicity if the queen lives in both of us and neither of us at the same time? (2017, p. 719).

Somewhere in the dance of power, it is up to the analyst to stop the psychotic spinning by taking the step to examine their own interiority for the location of the problem. I begin to look. I wonder: "Is it me? No, surely, it isn't me—I can't be the one with the problem, I'm the one suffering over here. She's the one who's constantly rejecting me." I begin to examine all the possible "diagnoses" as a defense against the core dyadic problem. With each rejection of me I feel unappreciated. Shards of her reality come firing across the consulting room threatening my sense of authority. I grapple with myself over the very idea that the analyst ultimately holds the authority anyway. Nonviolence teaches that power, the real power is the constant surrendering to an idea of love being the ultimate authority. Indeed, the ego has a very difficult time with the concept and constantly struggles with its own aggressive forces of nature in its metaphysical quest for freedom (war between dominance and submission), power and love.

Indeed, the urge to power may be the inducing substance of the dance which is destroying the soul of the work, and whose location (in her and/or in me) may also provide the compensatory healing. While the dance is inevitable, nonviolent consciousness can be the intruder who leans in, encouraging the analyst to check themselves, thus resisting the violence which threatens to destroy. The moments of recognition—that is, the meeting of the shadowed other—becomes the building block to a new consciousness. Through nonviolence we both come to understand that within each of us lay the persecutor and the persecuted, the master and the slave.

Through examination of my own defenses and the realization that I am experiencing that which Linda lives every day breaks through into the analytic field and seeps into me. At once, I feel guilty that I have been running from an essential healing component—connection through compassion. My ego's need to be the "good analyst" the one who is in charge, had interrupted the necessary moment-to-moment process of attunement, which she so desperately needed, and which she had rarely received in her life. I had to examine my own destructive urge to power, and yet, not fall for the idea that I am holistically, bad either.

She sits cross-legged on the couch chewing away at old resentments, hiding the fact that she longs for a meaningful relationship with her boss, whom she feels constantly derides her. She is confident that her boss is punishing her through an endless stream of audits and demands, and wonders if her boss does this because she suspects Linda's sexual preference. I inquire whether she has ever thought about asking her boss how she really feels about her; confront the issue, end the dance once and for all. She gives me that confused look, lifting her nose ever so slightly into the air and sniffs, indicating that she's been insulted. She raises her voice and snaps, "I told you she hates me. And, besides that, she's a Republican. They all hate gays." I hold the moment in stony silence. We stare each other down. I don't waste the long-awaited opportunity for consciousness. I pointedly state, "You sound like a racist right now." And then, like rapid machine gun fire, she spits it from her lips, "God, such you're a witch ... no, you're a witch-bitch." Silence thumps me on the nose, blowing her over with a feather. Before she can take it back, I say: "Really. Well, yes, I suppose you're right there ... a bitch I certainly can be, but as far as the witch goes, I thought she lived over there. In you." And so, finally, the bigoted, elitist, racist-based other comes striding in on its centuries-old horse stunning us both into a silence riddled with aggression, hatred, abuse and threats of annihilation; a personal and cultural legacy bored down into our DNA so deeply it simply can no longer be denied. It has been said.

Linda leaves the session in tears, the knowledge of her own bigotry finally unfurled on me. Splattered across the consulting room, humiliating her beyond words that matter. I am awash in a guilt that threatens to pull me under. I hear Freud's voice over my right shoulder: "I told you this was the impossible profession." Then I hear Jung over my left shoulder: "oh dear ... and just *what* are *you* going to do about the transference ... you know she hates you now." I find myself chastising both of them: "Oh, for God's sake, give it rest would you?"

While Linda had a fortified defensive structure, it is through her walls of stubbornness that my own interiority begins to shine. I find that in the transference Linda had begun sending me messages that I wasn't all that effective. After all, how did I *really know* what might be best for her? I didn't live her life. I hadn't suffered the labor pains of sexual identity, marginalization or her own uniquely painful experience of childhood abuse and neglect.

I begin to question my own feelings about my work with Linda. While I understand the process of projections, I also know that I have to look into my own soul and honestly explore my own inner bigot, racist. I find myself wondering: "Has Linda detected some hubris in me that wouldn't change? More importantly, "has she detected and hooked into some racist that lives deeply in me, clamping down for fear of rejection. Was I enacting her encapsulated position of introversion and hubris like she did at work?"

On the conscious level it seems as though Linda has been damaged by me. Two of King's tenets unfurl in my mind like ticker tape across the television news screen: The nonviolent practitioner does not harm his opponent spiritually, and the nonviolent activist accepts violence but never inflicts it. Over the course of the work, I know that I have been the recipient of many verbal attacks from Linda which would have been exceedingly easy to take personally (and I have), yet, I know that these attacks represent her defensive posturing designed to cover her pain. Over and over again, I have had to learn to work with my egoic projections in order to sink into a deeper understanding of what Linda wishes for rather than what she is defending against, and this process has enabled me to tolerate her projectiles of aggression, and accept them in the face of her resistances and desire to be loved and accepted. All because I hope that she will learn to trust me and eventually trust herself, allowing me to bring her back into the human fold of the communal love and acceptance from which she has felt alienated for so long.

I am also aware that it is her bruised ego, not her "self" that is damaged by the insight. Her procrustean attitude can only be cracked into when the brittle shell of her ego can be accessed, a new consciousness informing her life which has long been protected by her well-defended system. While other opportunities for ego dissolution had occurred throughout the treatment, it was only in this moment that Linda couldn't turn away. The accumulation of small encounters with her shadow; the coming together of her opposite halves, in dialogue through me, confronting and accepting some new truth, had finally opened up a channel deep enough for her ego to see through to another side of life, a view that was complete, filled with what she could be. Yes, she could hate, but somewhere the pain had to be experienced long enough, and deeply enough that the aggression could potentially be nonviolently transmuted. For both us, suffering had been redemptive for Linda. She was beginning to change.

In the following years a softness begins to reveal itself in Linda. It unfolds from her temperament through a particular patience alive within herself, *for* herself. She brings her judgmental tendencies into the consulting room, and through nonviolence, I peel them back exposing the prism of other possibilities that lie within her projections. While this seems like an uncooperative endeavor, it isn't. The encounters are infused with a strengthened trust, holding her fragility in a place of reverie between her and me. But, it is in her first confrontation with her boss that Linda experiences the depths of her projections.

When she finally gains the courage to ask for some time off, her boss not only congratulates her for taking care of herself but sends her flowers. This act of kindness releases a torrent of tears in the re-telling of the story, and introduces Linda to the compassionate inner master, which has been hidden within the folds of her injuries. As she builds upon these important milestones of self-awareness, psychic strength builds upon itself. The tactics emerge organically from me as the work progresses. Silence, meditation (reverie), encouragement, protesting (not falling back from a position of untruth) become evident in the work.

Months of work begin loosening up the wedges in Linda's rigid psychic paneling. But the depths of her anxiety will not fully dissipate until something significant shifts in the cultural complex of homosexuality. It was at this point in time when the Supreme Court issued a ruling in favor of gay marriage throughout the fifty-states. Part of the ruling states:

> No union is more profound than marriage, for it embodies the highest ideals of love, fidelity, devotion, sacrifice, and family. In forming a marital union, two people become something greater than they once were. [The challengers] ask for equal dignity in the eyes of the law. The Constitution grants them that right. (Chappell, 2015).

With the prejudicial confines of homosexuality giving way to liberation under the law, Linda feels safer in her life and at work. She finds out that a new hire at work is openly gay, which then gives her permission to openly identify as well. Finally, she can bring her partner out in the open as well. She can display their picture on her desk, as well as celebrate the holidays at each other's Christmas parties. Within the year Linda and her partner marry. She displays a new wedding ring with pride. I think of King's final tenet: "Nonviolence is based on the conviction that the universe is on the side of justice," and I am somewhat awe-inspired. While the world is riddled by injustices and evil, the codes of morality revealed through consciousness indicate that there is an order which emerges through the struggle with the inner forces of our nature. It is an order which seems to emerge both within ourselves and at the same time through our relationships with others. It is an expression of the Self's revelation.

While Linda sits across from me these days, smiling with her earrings bobbing in time with her head, I hear King's words: "All men are caught in an inescapable network of mutuality, tied to a single garment of destiny. Whatever affects one affects all indirectly. I can never be what I ought to be until you are what you ought to be, and you can never be what you ought to be until I am what I ought to be" (King, 2010, ix).

References

Benjamin, J. (1988). *The Bonds of Love: Psychoanalysis, Feminism and the Problem of Domination*. New York: Pantheon Books.

Chappell, B. (2015, June 26). *NPR.org*. Retrieved from National Public Radio KJZZ: https://www.npr.org/sections/thetwo-way/2015/06/26/417717613/supreme-cour t-rules-all-states-must-allow-same-sex-marriages.

Davies, Jody Messler, (2017). Whose Bad Objects are We Anyway? Repetition and Our Elusive Love Affair with Evil. *Psychoanalytic Dialogues*, pp. 711–732.

Jung, C. (1964/1970). *The Collected Works of C.G. Jung Volume 10, Civilization in Transition*. Princeton: Princeton University Press.

Jung, C. (1966). *The Collected Works of C.G. Jung, Volume 16, The Practice of Psychotherapy*. Princeton: Princeton University Press.

Kalsched, D. (2013). *Trauma and the Soul: A Psychospiritual Approach to Human Development and Its Interruption*. London, New York: Routledge.

King, M. L. (2010). *Strength to Love*. Minneapolis: Fortress Press.

Chapter 10

Where do we go from here?

The country experienced just five days of peace following the signing of the Voting Rights Act. The moment of national union and subsequent celebration had barely begun when the rebellions ensued. The first explosions occurred on August 11–16, 1965 when Watts, a suburb of Los Angeles, California, burned following a black parolee's altercation with police. "Six days of rioting, resulting in 34 deaths, over 1,000 injuries, nearly 4,000 arrests, and the destruction of property valued at $40 million" (The King Institute, 1965). This time, nonviolence could not hold back the flood of rage, and like a virus, the riots spread. The city of Chicago broke open from a similar altercation between an African American and law enforcement official, leading to a four-day riot, between July12–15, 1966. It didn't take long for a huge portion of the country to respond to these rebellions in kind. In 1967 alone, race riots occurred in Tampa, Florida; Cincinnati, Ohio; Atlanta, Georgia; Newark, Plainfield, and New Brunswick, New Jersey; and Detroit, Michigan. On the night of Dr. King's assassination 110 riots broke out in cities across the nation (The King Institute, 1965).

The assassinations of Medgar Evers, Malcom X, and finally King peeled back the archetypal defenses within the complex long enough to reveal the deep trauma of racism and its pathological constructs. According to Marten W. DeVries, in *Traumatic Stress, The Effects of Overwhelming Experience on Mind, Body, and Society*, cultural upheaval and trauma causes a degeneration in social systems which heretofore protects its citizenry.

> Culture is supposed to render life predictable. When the cultural defense mechanisms are lost, individuals are left on their own to achieve emotional control. Traumas that occur in the context of social upheavals, such as revolutions, civil wars, and uprootings, create profound discontinuity in the order and predictability that culture has brought to daily life and social situations. When this occurs, traditional systems break down and a conservative element often takes hold. Ethnicity, nationalism, tribalism and fundamentalism become means of survival (van der Kolk et al, 2007, p. 407).

In such an environment, when the government fails to uphold the cultural and social structures, the tribe or party becomes a psychic skin of protection against real and perceived annihilation. During the civil rights movement both sides of the split would have considered their lives threatened because each side did not see change as archetypally present. When this occurs the culture is shattered. Any induction of change into a traumatized and fragile culture will constellate archetypal defenses. As such, King's movement deeply rocked the status quo, caused tremendous upheaval within the collective unconscious but provided an opening for the adaptive change the collective unconscious demanded.

The civil rights movement demonstrated that when cultural moral corruption is challenged it is critical that the psychological container within the process be carefully implemented and maintained, sometimes over the course of years. Selma created such a container, but with carefully constructed social and political maneuverings. Selma became the tipping point for the change that had been unconsciously building over the course of ten years. The zeitgeist flipped in moments, a confluence of individual, cultural and collective factors intersecting in a moment in time.

Progressive cultural movements are often defined by a symphonic flow-counterflow of energy, each apex shaped by a violent upheaval. Any real change requires a consistent, persistent pressure on the oppressive forces which feed any split, so that within the folds of progress, some form of consciousness survives. Whether applied individually or collectively, the eightfold path of nonviolence enables said pressure to induce variant levels of conscious change.

A nonviolent ethos emphasizes that forgiveness must hold the hand of patience. Nonviolent consciousness in and of itself can be a violent process which requires a specific understanding and tolerance for psychological and emotional pain, a difficult recipe in today's electrically charged social and political environment. America is seemingly in a state of Exile, separated within itself, becoming alienated from the rest of the world. King's last book *Where do we go from Here? Chaos to Community* (1967), consisted of his vision for the future of America; thus, the title for this chapter. It seemed fitting to begin here again. King reminded his readers of the accomplishments of nonviolence, both great and small, as well as the work that still needed to be done. His nonviolent philosophy and history showed that much can be gained through progressive spiritual warfare. As the civil rights movement demonstrated, the seeds of nonviolent consciousness constellated within the individual has outcomes that cannot be measured in linear space and time.

Nonviolence in Selma changed the face of today's America to include substantive progress for African Americans in the attainment of the vote. On the 50th anniversary of Bloody Sunday, C. T. Vivien, activist, minister and close confidante of King's, emphasized the importance of embracing the story of Selma and its pivotal role in the African American and American narrative.

"Everything has changed. What you couldn't do (then), you now can do. What your children were never going to be able to do, they can now do, and are doing" (CNN Films, 2015, 4:23). Joanne Bland, an activist who was eleven years old on Bloody Sunday, stated, "I think it's very important that all people know where this country has been. We made it (Selma) as a stepping-stone to the future" (CNN Films, 2015, 4:50). Andrew Young, activist, politician and confidante of King's, doubted that King would have believed any of today's achievements could have been made possible.

> If I had said to Martin 'I'm going to be the Mayor of Atlanta one day, or the Ambassador at the U.N. (United Nations), he would have said, 'boy, you're sick, sit down and have a cool drink of water.' We were really doing something so that our children would have a better life ... Most of us thought we would never make it to 40 ... (we were) all in our 30's at the time. (CNN Films, 2015)

Similarly, John Lewis would exit Selma carrying his activism into politics where he would become a U.S. Congressman, re-elected six times over. And yet, there are the dismal figures: "Black families in America earn just $57.30 for every $100 in income earned by white families, according to the Census Bureau's Current Population Survey. For every $100 in white family wealth, black families hold just $5.04" (Badge, 2017). Institutionalized racism continues to oppress minorities in businesses, prisons, schools, and politics.

Activist James Baldwin wrote,

> One can only face in others what one can face in oneself. This confrontation depends on the measure of our wisdom and compassion. This energy is all that one finds in the rubble of vanished civilizations, and the only hope for ours. (1961, p. 14)

Because Whites sit in a historically privileged position, most are unable to understand the existential realities of racism for black Americans. Moreover, because many Whites can't empathize with that which they are not, as in the severe poverty and oppression many Blacks experience, they remain separated from their racist shadow, and the ways in which racism may become enacted in their everyday lives. Many Whites would not publicly admit that they are as exhausted of being made to face the race problem as Blacks are sick of experiencing it. White fatigue and impatience are symptoms of the hubris, which is so difficult to treat. Between the two positions exists a chasm of disparity in empathy, understanding and relatedness. The disconnect keeps us from grieving the trauma, the essential step in healing the divide. Thus, it is even more imperative that the issue continues to be negotiated, personally and collectively, or at our own peril, as Baldwin warned.

The collective effects of racism have created cultural Post-Traumatic Stress Disorder (PTSD), a long-term maladaptive response to a cultural trauma (Van der Kolk et al, 2007, p. 401). As research shows, a traumatized culture in disorder, regresses, becoming more tribal and hierarchical, opening the door to tyranny. Marten DeVries stated:

> Ethnicity, nationalism, tribalism, and fundamentalism become means of survival; all of these are regressive moves to release individuals behaviorally and ideologically from an extreme complexity that cannot be managed or used more productively. When culture as the identity giver fails, other models of identity formation and social group formation take its place. The roles and status that had previously organized the system may have no further meaning...." (Van der Kolk et al., 2007, p. 407).

Our inability to collectively process the grief petrifies the cultural complex, feeds the split, fortifying the positions of those on either side. The lack of cultural containment keeps the aggression repressed, unavailable for alchemical transformation through nonviolent means.

Our early history of Native American genocide and PTSD suffered among its people provide the starkest reality for collective moral reflection. The Native American way of life sacralizes the relationship between the human and natural worlds; their genocidal history the metaphor for how we have become so sick and provides the clues as to how we may return to ourselves. Anthony Stephens, in his book *Archetype Revisited* (2015) stated, Jung "believed modern man to be sick because he had lost his customary access to the traditional resources of his culture: the cure, therefore, lay in enabling him to establish contact with the resources inherent in his own nature" (Stephens, 2015, p. 39). When the dominant cultural formation is pathological, growth is restricted. When growth is restricted, we have to leave home.

As essentially tribal beings, maintaining a healthy connection to a tribe in service of a diversely defined culture serves the tribe and the health of the nation. Collective healing can occur through honoring diversity and supporting tribal and ethnic identity. For example, in the Native American community drum ceremonies such as the gourd dance, gave warriors the means to cathect the trauma of war once they laid down their arms, and through communal support, reintegrate back into society. According to Marten DeVries:

> the gourd dance served as a means to work out their frustrations. At the end of the Vietnam War, when Native American veterans came home, they were again warriors who had turned in their weapons. They were sitting around in cities and towns not knowing what to do, drinking,

often getting into trouble, and lacking a sense of orientation. The gourd dance, with its unique pulsating circular rhythm and the social activities surrounding it, reemerged as a means of reestablishing orientation ... In the group process the 'sufferer' is gradually transformed into a healer; in these self-help groups, in striking contrast to orthodox professional medical models, evil is somehow converted into a virtue. (Van der Kolk et al., 2017, pp. 408–409)

Similarly, the Selma marches were contained through a nonviolent ethos defined by prayer, song, scripture and the cathexis of transgenerational racial trauma in the presence of community within Brown's Chapel in Selma. These meetings became healing rituals in the face of oppressive conditions. Working with psychological and emotional suffering through a deep connection to one's nature (unconscious world) in the presence of the community has the potential to heal. It revitalizes the individual's sense of purpose and restores one's connection to the community. To restore harmony and make contact with the Self, one needs to be able to celebrate one's cultural and tribal heritage, ancestral lineage, and the communal experience of being diversely American. This deeper connection also involves the witnessing and suffering of our American history together.

Communal witnessing is a form of *ahimsa*, the psychological and emotional containment of suffering. Activist Fabrizio Petri, in his article "Gandhi, Jung and Nonviolence Today" (2014), emphasized James Hillman's idea of cultivating Anima and its potential to heal the world's soul. *Ahimsa* cultivates Anima or soul; the psyche's capacity to produce meaningful experiences that are "soul-making" (Petri, 2014, pp. 12). The cultivation of nonviolence in one's life holistically nourishes the world due to our universal connection to each other and nature, which cannot be separated. Hillman believed that the world soul needed nurturing and begins with the individual. Here, Petri discusses Hillman's point of view:

the suffering of the individual cannot be separated any longer from the suffering of the world. Hillman understood how much of his patients' distress was linked to the afflictions of the environment in which they lived, even if such a link was subconscious. It is a vision that brings Anima's potentialities to the fore. To save yourself meant giving back its soul to the world, starting with changing one's attitude towards it ... Hillman's effort is to rebuild a lost link between the human soul and the world outside. We simply must stop viewing the world as a dead reality, existing for our use and desire. Instead, we must see the world in a psychological light, as provided by 'Anima Mundi.' Giving back Anima to the world is to understand that we depend on it, that we cannot anymore overcome our suffering without conceiving a new relationship with it (Petri, 2014, p. 12).

A nonviolent practice is thus a feminine practice that involves the essential experience of nonviolence as the transformative substance of violence. Selma demonstrated that the cultivation of consciousness can occur through other means, like communal connection and the carrying of opposites for and with the group. During the Southern nonviolent campaigns there were those who effectively contributed to the greater good by holding the tactical end of the spectrum, while others held the philosophical stance. However, it was the union of both that contributed to the communal change. The power of community building inspires moral acuity because it tames the individual ego, inspiring the individual to a higher purpose.

King emphasized collective and social activism as a means of taming the urges to power through brotherhood. In *The Papers of Martin Luther King, Jr.*, King states: "The real problem is that through our scientific genius we've made of the world a neighborhood but through our moral and spiritual genius we've failed to make of it a brotherhood" (Clayborne Carson, 1994, p. 27).

As history has proved, mass movements that develop in the face of oppressive societies can produce mass destruction brought on by faulty values espoused by morally bankrupt leaders. This phenomenon is ushered in through individuals who have lower levels of consciousness than others, or where developmental object constancy has foreclosed on the capacity for self-reflection. Those with little insight into their own behavior are more likely to be slowly seduced by tyrannical personalities. According to Murray Stein in his book *Encountering Evil, Jung on Evil*:

> A strong influx of archetypal energy and content from the unconscious shades the light of ego consciousness and interferes with a person's ability to make moral distinctions. Now ordinary moral categories and the ego's ethical attainments are easily over-ridden in the name of a 'higher' (certainly stronger) values. And when these dubious higher values have become the group norm, individual and collective shadows have found a secure playground. This is how evil is unleashed on a mass scale; it is individual shadow added to shadow and then raised to the square power by group consensus, permission and pressure. (1995, p. 13)

The health of a community and culture lies in the hands of the individual's capacity to understand the ego's vulnerability and its instinctual urge to power, particularly in the face of perceived threat and violence. In order to tame the ego, the individual must have the wherewithal to challenge perceived truths, or projections through an objective search for the truth; while also holding aggression in check through nonviolent means. Consciousness lies within the folds of the inner–outer conflict, its organic unfolding within the individual and culture a true mystery and an inherent part of our nature.

The revelation of shadow, an integral aspect of the development of consciousness, is also a deep mystery.

Jung understood the role of shadow and the cautionary tale that shadow provides. He warned that World War II was coming when he began to see the theme running through the psyches of his German patients. In his book *Civilization in Transition*, Jung discussed this phenomenon:

> The archetypes I had observed (in dreams) expressed primitivity, violence, and cruelty. When I had seen enough of such cases I turned my attention to the peculiar state of mind then prevailing in Germany. I could only see signs of depression and a great restlessness, but this did not ally my suspicions ... The onslaught of primitive forces was more or less universal. The only difference lay in the German mentality itself, which proved to be more susceptible because of the marked proneness of the Germans to mass psychology. Moreover, defeat and social disaster had increased the herd instinct in Germany, so that it became more and more probable that Germany would be the first victim among the Western nations—victim of a mass movement brought about by an upheaval of forces lying dormant in the unconscious, ready to break through all moral barriers. (Jung, 1964/1970, para. 444–457)

In the America of 2020, the racist split has become more pronounced and is seemingly transmuting from race to politics, the Democrats and Republicans becoming what in medieval Europe was the war between the Protestants and Catholics. The split is fed by a confluence of individual, familial, cultural and technological influences foreclosing on our capacity for self-reflection, instinctively available within our human being, but deeply damaging our human becoming. Collective uprisings are the harbingers for moral reconciliation. The women's march of 2016 consisted of a collective upheaval of outrage against the forces of leadership which were in direct opposition to the betterment of the greater good of the country. The collective unconscious expressed itself through the voices of the people, demanding a moral reconciliation within, beginning with the office of the Presidency. With 2020 approaching, the collective reconciliation still hangs in the balance, the collective developmental crisis still unresolved.

King urged us to look beyond just actions. He bid us explore the moorings of our soul, his message as much alive today as it was then. He stated,

> The greatest need of civilization today is not political security; the greatest need of civilization today is not a well-rounded United Nations Organization; the greatest need of civilization today is not a multiplicity of materials goods; the greatest need of civilization today is not the superb genius of science as important as it is; the greatest need of civilization today is moral progress. (Clayborne Carson, 1994, p. 86)

While nonviolence may not always work, history reveals a longstanding record of nonviolent campaigns preventing and ending wars. French novelist Anatole France wrote: "War will disappear only when men shall take no part whatever in violence and shall be ready to suffer every persecution that their abstention will bring them. It is the only way to abolish war" (Kurlansky, 2006, p. 182). King and Gandhi consistently echoed the same message. Only months shy of his assassination, King admitted that the dream he had for the nation had turned into somewhat of a nightmare after Selma (NBC News, 1967, 22:33). However, his faith in nonviolence never wavered. "Occasionally in life, one develops a conviction so precious and meaningful that he will stand on it till the end. That is what I have found in nonviolence" (King, 1967, p. 69).

As history has shown, violence and nonviolence consist of a partnership whose outcomes of peace, militancy, or violence are determined from within the psyches of those at the epicenter of conflicts, with consciousness determining the outcome. Therefore, persistent and patient work on one's psyche affect the outcome. Edward Edinger recited the Bible and Yahweh's promise of peace for those living a conscious life.

> You know in the Old Testament, in Genesis when God is about to destroy Sodom and Gomorrah for its sins, Abraham remonstrates with God and says, 'What if we've got some righteous people in those cities, what if there are fifty?' And Yahweh says, 'Well, then I'll save the city if there are fifty.' And Abraham works him all the way down to ten—What if there are ten?' And Yahweh says, 'I'll save the city if there are ten.' Abraham doesn't want to push his luck too far, so he stops there. But it's too beyond the realm of possibility that just *one* person might be enough to preserve the world. I would suggest that you entertain the idea, and furthermore, consider that perhaps *you* are the one (1995, p. 326).

Cultivating a conscious life is going to be critical in our capacity to survive the future rumblings of world change and the chaos that is unfolding. While Jung understood the shadow, he also provided the map to the inner world where the self resides. The map points towards one's holistically involved relationship with the divine, something outside of one's immediate ego-oriented experience. For some, the ego-self relationship can be cultivated through psychoanalysis where one's dream life and imagination can begin to transform the ego's urges to power. On another level, more simply defined, one can tame the ego's urges to power through a practice of nonviolence. According to Petri (2014):

> While it's easy to speculate about utopian nonviolent policies, it is far more difficult to deny the factual implications of such a value when we realize that it can belong to every human hearth, under every sky; when

we know that Ahimsa can become attitude—and the tool in the hands— of every human being if each one of us were committed to cultivate his or her own Anima. (p. 11)

As the world grows smaller from global warming, migration will increase, food sources will decline, technology will dominate the employment landscape and violence will ensue, reconfiguring the world order, unless nonviolent forces rise to mediate the threat of annihilation. Indeed, global warming may be our next Selma. Nonviolent action will begin with the individual leading the way to the many.

References

Badger, E. (2017, September 18). Whites Have Huge Wealth Edge Over Blacks (but Don't Know It), *New York Times*. Retrieved from https://www.nytimes.com/interactive/2017/09/18/upshot/black-white-wealth-gap-perceptions.html?searchResultPosition=1.

Baldwin, J. (1961). *Nobody Knows My Name*. New York: Random House.

Central News Network (CNN) (2015, March 7). Central News Network-Selma 50 Years Later, *CNN.com*. Retrieved from http://www.cnn.com/videos/us/2015/03/04/voices-of-selma-50th-anniversary.cnn.

Clayborne Carson, S. E. (1994). *The Papers of Martin Luther King, Jr., Volume II, Rediscovering Precious Values, July 1951–1955*. Berkley, Los Angeles, London: University of California Press.

Edinger, Edward (1995). *The Mysterium Lectures: A Journey through C.G. Jung's Mysterium Coniunctionis*. Toronto: Inner City Books.

Jung. C. G. (1964/1970). *The Collected Works of C.G. Jung*, Volume 10, Civilization in Transition. Princeton: Princeton University Press.

King, J., M. L. (1967). *Where do we go From Here? Chaos to Community*. Boston: Beacon Press (Kindle Edition).

Kurlansky, M. (2006). *Nonviolence: the History of a Dangerous Idea*. New York: Random House Publishing Group.

NBC News (1967). Interviewer, Sander Vanocur. Retrieved from https://www.youtube.com/watch?v=2xsbt3a7K-8&t=1388s.

Petri, F. (Summer 2014). Gandhi, Jung and Nonviolence Today: The Relevance of the Feminine in the Network Society. *IIC Quarterly*, 41(1), 7–18.

Stein, M. (1995). *Encountering Jung: Jung on Evil, 1995 Selected and Introduced by Murray Stein*. Princeton: Princeton University Press.

Stephens, A. (2015). *Archetype Revisited*. London, New York: Routledge.

The King Institute (1965, August 11–16). *Stanford University: The Martin Luther King, Jr. Research and Education Institute*. Retrieved from https://kinginstitute.stanford.edu:https://kinginstitute.stanford.edu/encyclopedia/watts-rebellion-los-angeles.

van der Kolk, A. B., McFarlane, A. C. and Weisaeth, L. (2007). *Traumatic Stress The Effects of Overwhelming Experience on Mind, Body, and Society*. New York: Guilford Press.

Index

For Product Safety Concerns and Information please contact our EU
representative GPSR@taylorandfrancis.com
Taylor & Francis Verlag GmbH, Kaufingerstraße 24, 80331 München, Germany

www.ingramcontent.com/pod-product-compliance
Lightning Source LLC
Chambersburg PA
CBHW050527270326
41926CB00015B/3112